SENATOR
HATTIE
CARAWAY

AN ARKANSAS LEGACY

Dr. Nancy Hendricks

FOREWORD BY
SENATOR BLANCHE LINCOLN

THE
History
PRESS

Published by The History Press
Charleston, SC 29403
www.historypress.net

Front cover: U.S. Senate Collection.

Unless otherwise noted, all images appear courtesy of the author.

First published 2013

Manufactured in the United States

ISBN 978.1.60949.968.6

Library of Congress CIP data applied for.

CONTENTS

U.S. Senate Collection.

FOREWORD

During Women's History Month of 2005, I had the honor to stand before the United States Senate in tribute to a very special woman, Hattie Ophelia Wyatt Caraway. On January 12, 1932, this Arkansan became the first woman ever elected to the Senate.

When I think of the life of Hattie Caraway, I think of a life devoted to the family, state and country that she loved so deeply. Those who knew her were drawn to her endearing sense of humor, her gentle and dignified manner and her warmth. The example she set, both personally and professionally, has always been an inspiration to me. As the second woman to serve Arkansas in the U.S. Senate, I felt a special bond with Hattie and was humbled to follow in her footsteps.

Though she first came to the Senate following the death of her husband, a historic election allowed her to achieve what no woman had ever achieved: an elected seat in the U.S. Senate. It was not only a testament to the open-mindedness and fairness of the people of Arkansas but also to the kind of woman Hattie Caraway was.

With a firm belief that "the time has passed when a woman should be placed in a position and kept there only while someone else is being groomed for the job," she stood boldly in the face of overwhelming odds to campaign for a full Senate term. During the 1932 campaign with the flamboyant Huey Long barnstorming the state on her behalf, Depression-stricken Arkansans who were enduring unemployment, poverty and low farm prices began to see Hattie Caraway for who she was, an honorable friend and neighbor who would remain their advocate. At the polls, the people of Arkansas stood by Hattie in overwhelming numbers, doubling the votes of her nearest rival and carrying sixty-one of Arkansas' seventy-five counties. Then in 1938, she made history again by becoming the first women to be reelected to the Senate.

Certainly, it was rare for "Silent Hattie" to participate actively in debate or deliver a speech to the chamber. She was weary of politicians who placed a higher priority on hearing their own voice than working on behalf of the people they were elected to represent, once remarking, "It's funny how they talk on after we've all made up our minds." Senator Caraway took her responsibilities as a legislator seriously and built a reputation among her colleagues as a woman of integrity who showed a determination to faithfully champion the interests of Arkansas above everything else.

Although she passed away in 1950, her impact is still felt in the institution she served and by all of us who found inspiration in the life she led. Her lasting legacy lives on in those who are—and who will be—inspired by her example to follow the road she so boldly paved.

When I had the honor to serve in the Senate, the nine female senators all contributed to a book called *Nine and Counting*, which was published in 2001. As optimistic as we were, did we really imagine that within slightly more than a decade, there would be *twenty* women of the Senate, as there are today?

Hattie would be proud.

It is up to us to continue the progress she made and to urge a new generation to follow the heroic example set by her and so many other pioneering women. When I think of Hattie Caraway, I think of a quote that I carried with me throughout my first Senate campaign: "If I can hold on to my sense of humor and a modicum of dignity, I shall have a wonderful time running for office whether I get there or not."

Well, Hattie, you got there. In the process, your humor carried you through and your dignity earned you the affection of generations who are inspired to follow in your footsteps. Despite whatever barriers that those of us who followed may encounter or traditions that we must overcome, each of us has what Hattie did not—a woman who led the way. That woman's name is Hattie Caraway.

I am proud that she is from my home state of Arkansas, and I am proud to call her one of my heroes.

—Senator Blanche Lincoln

Acknowledgements

Sincere thanks to:

Dr. Brady Banta, Archivist, Arkansas State University Archives and
Special Collections

Jimmy Bryant, Director of Archives and Special Collections,
University of Central Arkansas

Amy Elizabeth Burton, Assistant Curator, United States Senate

Malissa Davis, Library Technician, Arkansas State University Archives and
Special Collections

Mrs. Betty Caraway Hill

Representative Donna Hutchinson

Dr. Betty Koed, Associate Historian, United States Senate

Senator Blanche Lambert Lincoln

Julie MacDonald, Curator, Arkansas State University Museum

Heather Moore, Photo Historian, U.S. Senate Historical Office

Christen Thompson, Commissioning Editor, The History Press

Singing the Praises of "Silent Hattie"

Hattie Caraway has been part of my life as long as I can remember. My father knew her during World War II and shared stories of the first woman elected as a U.S. senator, serving from 1932 to 1945. Along with touching personal anecdotes, such as how she took the time to help find his lost air force ring and to learn about his hometown of New York City, he stressed what an accomplishment it was for her to be the first woman elected—and reelected—to the United States Senate.

But I never truly understood the enormity of her achievement until entering public service myself with Texas governor Ann Richards more than a half century later. Even at the dawn of the twenty-first century, a woman in politics was not an easy role. Caraway may have been called "Silent Hattie," but I knew I wanted to help sing her praises.

I had written a play based on her 1932 campaign with Huey Long called *Miz Caraway and the Kingfish*, but as the title suggests, it was as much about Long as Caraway. Long was well documented. Sadly, few of Hattie Caraway's papers have survived. Other than her journal written primarily in 1932, there was very little from more than a dozen years of her service in the Senate.

Then, boxes of papers from the estate of former Arkansas State University president V.C. Kays were donated to the ASU Archives by his son. Included were letters to and from Hattie Caraway. It turned out to be a treasure trove.

Through those letters, her conscientious work as a senator can be seen. They clearly show the effort she put in to helping her home state, and the visible results of those efforts, many of which still stand today as her unheralded legacy.

Caraway's granddaughter, Betty Caraway Hill, confirmed that very few of Senator Caraway's papers existed anywhere. Therefore, despite the widely held belief that Caraway was quiet and ineffectual as a senator, the Kays papers show that she accomplished far more during the Depression and World War II than has been acknowledged.

A similar collection came to light at the University of Central Arkansas, confirming her achievements there.

Along with other demands on her time as a senator, we see firsthand how Caraway lobbied such daunting federal agencies as the Public Works Administration, Reconstruction Finance Corporation and Department of War on behalf of people back home. With her help, buildings were constructed through federal funding—for the first time—on Arkansas college campuses during the depths of the Depression. These buildings doubled—even tripled—campus size. Many are still heavily used today.

One of the most valuable things about Caraway's letters was seeing her personal thoughts. She comes alive, and a complex picture emerges. She is instrumental not only in securing complex building projects but also helping individual young people go to college. She took on the fearsome Department of War to secure military installations in Arkansas, but she also worried about eating too much.

Hattie Caraway entered the Senate as an outsider, but she got things done. She was grateful for her annual $10,000 senatorial salary and did not seek either self-aggrandizement or personal enrichment. She even felt bad accepting a prize from a perfume company.

Most of all, she never forgot the people back home. Perhaps by illuminating her achievements, we won't forget her, either.

Chapter 1

MEET HATTIE CARAWAY

"Write Senator Caraway. She will help you, if she can."

Visitors to the U.S. Capitol building in the 1930s would have been surprised to see someone described as one of the most visible women in America in a most unlikely place. In those days, the private restroom just off the Senate chamber was labeled "Senators," which meant males only. The lone woman senator was forced to leave the Senate, traverse the long corridors of the Capitol, mingle with the crowds and utilize the public facilities used by hundreds of tourists. She may or may not have been surprised to learn that not until 1993, some sixty years later, did female senators have a restroom of their own.

The little woman dressed all in black could have been someone's visiting grandmother whose only elected office was secretary of a small-town women's club. Indeed, that's exactly what she was before she carved a place in the history books.

Hattie Wyatt Caraway of Jonesboro, Arkansas, was the first woman elected to the United States Senate. She was a senator from 1932–45 and was often called "Silent Hattie" because she did not make the ponderous speeches her male colleagues were known for. But while she may not have been a legislative powerhouse, she never forgot the people who elected her.

She often voted with her heart, remembering where she came from and what ordinary Americans were suffering during the Depression. When a moratorium on foreign war debts was proposed, she voted against it, feeling that our country should not forgive the obligations of foreign nations when

Senator Hattie Caraway with gavel.

America's farm families who couldn't pay *their* debts were being evicted from their homes.

She publicly declared that she voted as "Dad" would have done, meaning her late husband Thad Caraway. Having been a farmhand as a boy, Thad fought in Congress for Arkansas' poor white farmers. Hattie's votes aided their cause as she presumed Thad would have done.

And she voted with a kind of homespun logic, as when dairy states sponsored a bill to prohibit butter substitutes such as the new "oleomargarine" from being used in federal agencies, including St. Elizabeth's Hospital for the Insane near Washington. Her stance was simple: "I feel that crazy people have as much right to butter as sane ones."

Welcome Discovery

She never forgot the people back home and worked tirelessly on their behalf, earning a reputation as a quiet but effective representative of her state during the Great Depression and World War II. An undisputed saying in Arkansas during the 1930s and '40s was, "Write Senator Caraway. She will help you, if she can."

Yet, relatively few papers remain to offer evidence of Hattie Caraway's term in office over those two tumultuous decades. There was Caraway's uneven journal, which she wrote primarily during 1932 with some apparent thought to possible publication. On February 11, 1932, she wrote, "The following written after 1st week in Senate. Copied here to preserve for the world," and the next month, "This is pretty personal little journal, but I will edit before it is published—if ever. Doesn't it sound big to think or talk of having something published?"

But otherwise, little documentation exists from her senatorial tenure. The scarcity of documents has been attributed to various causes. Some say they languish somewhere in a sub-basement at the Library of Congress, misplaced, uncatalogued and forgotten. Some say a few ended up in the attic of her loyal chief of staff, Garrett Whiteside, though he passed away three years before she did. Others say they may have been destroyed by a senator who held a grudge against her for an election defeat.

Caraway's granddaughter, Betty Caraway Hill, stated to the author that she does not feel any of those theories are likely and thinks Hattie herself may have had them destroyed. Said Mrs. Hill, "They could have been accidentally thrown out when she got sick. My dad [Hattie Caraway's son Forrest] said she destroyed the papers because 'they were not important.'"

Therefore, uncovering a cache of previously unknown Caraway documents is a welcome and important discovery. Correspondence between Caraway and V.C. Kays, founding president of Arkansas State University in Jonesboro, is a rare gift for those interested in Hattie Caraway. It is currently housed in the ASU Archives, courtesy of Victor Hale (Buddy) Kays, who preserved his father's papers.

Each of the twelve large document files in the collection contains approximately one hundred letters and other documents, totaling more than 1,200. Given Caraway's dozen years in the Senate, that averages about one hundred a year, or one every three days to Kays alone, some written by hand. They show how her help provided nine new buildings with federal funds for

Mature Hattie Caraway.

the small campus, allowing it to grow in both students and programs until it was only the second institution in the state to attain university status.

A similar collection of letters between Caraway and University of Central Arkansas president Heber McAlister can be found at the UCA Archives in Conway. Jimmy Bryant, director of UCA's Archives and Special Collections said, "Senator Caraway assisted UCA (Arkansas State Teachers College at the time) in navigating through the system and receiving the proper financing."

As with ASU, the state of Arkansas did not contribute any funds for buildings at UCA. Caraway's efforts tripled the size of the UCA campus. At both institutions, many of those buildings are still used today.

Her correspondence reveals Caraway to be a tireless public servant determined to learn quickly, fight her way through the daunting federal bureaucracy and serve the people of her state. It proves that Hattie Caraway is worthy of respect rather than being dismissed as ineffectual.

CURIOSITY

However, as the years passed, she was indeed often footnoted as ineffectual. Hattie Caraway became a curiosity, if she was remembered at all. By 1993, she was included as one of the oddities in a book called *The Mayflower Murderer and Other Forgotten Firsts in American History*. The "little widow woman," as the book repeatedly calls her, is numbered among two dozen other vignettes, including the first American counterfeiter and the inventor of chewing gum.

Even in her Senate years, Caraway understood that people saw her that way. George Creel, in the 1937 article "The Woman Who Holds her Tongue" in *Collier's* magazine, said, "The one and only thing that ever ruffles Mrs. Caraway's serenity is to be viewed as a curiosity. 'Sometimes,' she confesses, 'I'm really afraid that tourists are going to poke me with their umbrellas. And yet there's no sound reason why women, if they have the time and ability, shouldn't sit with men on city councils, in state legislatures or in the House and Senate. Particularly ability!'"

Diane Kincaid's 1979 book, *Silent Hattie Speaks*, shed light on Caraway through her sketchy journal and especially through Kincaid's scholarly annotations. Ten years later, David Malone's *Hattie and Huey: An Arkansas Tour* vividly brought the colorful 1932 campaign to life.

On July 22, 1984, the *Arkansas Democrat* ran a lengthy piece on Hattie Caraway. That was the year that Geraldine Ferraro ran for vice president on the national Democratic ticket, once again ushering in an alleged "Year of the Woman," a warmed-over catchphrase that has been reheated many times hence.

While for the most part not uncomplimentary, the piece included an undated clipping from the *Democrat* files with a cartoon of Caraway. The item was entitled "Strange as it Seems," by Elsie Hix, who wrote the popular national strip from 1948 to 1963. In addition to pointing out that "members of the cat family are the only clawed animals who do not walk on their claws," the piece included the following: "Hattie Caraway, Arkansas legislator and first woman senior Senator in U.S. history, was also the first woman elected to the Senate by popular vote, first woman chairman of a Senate committee, first woman to conduct a Senate hearing, and first woman to preside over the Senate."

So while Senator Hattie Caraway was remembered, it was as something of a curiosity on par with the animal kingdom.

Which therefore begs the question: who was she?

Chapter 2

WIFE, MOTHER, WIDOW

1878–1931

"No one will ever know how much we miss him."

Hattie Ophelia Wyatt was born on February 1, 1878, just one decade removed from the Civil War. Even her name is misleading. Some sources cite the original spelling of her first name as "Hatty." As for her middle name, Caraway's granddaughter relates the story she heard among family members that her grandmother's full given name was simply Hattie (or Hatty) Wyatt, but as a girl, she decided to add "Ophelia."

Her parents were William Carroll Wyatt (1818–1901), a farmer and shopkeeper, and his second wife, Lucy Mildred Burch Wyatt (1842–1922). William Wyatt's family had come to Tennessee from North Carolina around 1800. He was first married to Harriett O'Guinn; their surviving children, Hattie's half-siblings, were William, Charlie, Francis, Mollie, Laura and Ludie.

Following the death of Harriett, William Wyatt married Lucy. They became the parents of George Mizell Wyatt, Walter Eugene Wyatt (known as "Dick"), Moselle "Mosie" Wyatt (later Mrs. Shell Abbott) and Hattie.

Hattie was born on the family farm near the community of Bakerville, Tennessee, in Humphreys County. The county lies on the western edge of Middle Tennessee and borders Dickson County, where Hattie would later go to school.

Her father, William, was age sixty when Hattie was born; mother Lucy was thirty-six. When Hattie was four years old, the family moved to nearby Hustburg, also in Humphreys County. While a historical marker commemorating Hattie

Young Hattie Wyatt Caraway.

was unveiled there in 2003, Humphreys County became better known for Hurricane Mills, the home of country star Loretta Lynn.

The Wyatts were a family of modest means. William made a living through farming and running a small general store. However, Hattie, along with her sister Mosie, was able to obtain an education beyond the one-room schoolhouses common to that area at the time. Most nineteenth-century women of her generation were unable to do so, especially those growing up on a family farm in the rural South so soon after the Civil War.

Her granddaughter said, "According to family lore, Hattie wanted something better than the farm. She struck a bargain with an aunt that if she maintained good grades and good behavior, the aunt would pay for her schooling, which she did."

Hattie's destination was Dickson Normal School, also known as Dickson Normal College. Located in neighboring Dickson County, the school had been founded in 1885. Normal schools, as they were known at the time, trained graduates to become teachers in local high schools. Their mission was to establish teaching standards or norms, hence the name. Most such schools were later called teachers' colleges; at the time, they were basically equivalent to today's high schools.

In 1892 at age fourteen, Hattie began attending Dickson, graduating four years later with a Bachelor of Arts degree. Some subjects taught at the school included Greek, Latin, mathematics, science, bookkeeping, elocution, history, geography, penmanship and physical education. The school became a four-year county high school in 1919; its brick building was demolished in 1964.

Hattie's granddaughter believes that the Wyatt family farm in Humphreys County is currently under water due to the development of the Tennessee Valley Authority (TVA), built in part to control the regular flooding that devastated farms in that region. She said, "My grandmother was well aware of what floods did to farmers and took that on as part of her Senate work. She was also aware that a lack of education, especially for women, meant being trapped on the farm, and she tried to help others in that situation. While not what we might call a 'feminist,' she was very much into equal pay for equal work."

WHEN HATTIE MET THADDEUS

Upon graduation from Dickson Normal in 1896, Hattie taught school for several years. While at Dickson, she had met fellow student Thaddeus Horatius Caraway, originally from Spring Hill, Missouri, and later of Carroll County, Tennessee. Thad worked his way through school picking cotton and laboring in a sawmill. Like Hattie Wyatt, after graduation in 1896, he taught school for several years while he studied the law. Thad eventually established a legal practice in 1900 at the small town of Lake City in Craighead County, Arkansas.

Newlywed Thad Caraway. *Courtesy Caraway family.*

After marrying in 1902, when Hattie was age twenty-four, they moved to Jonesboro, Arkansas, the county seat of Craighead County. She was a farm wife who managed the small cotton plantation they acquired outside town while Thad climbed the political ladder. After establishing a Jonesboro law practice and serving as prosecuting attorney for the Second Judicial District, Thad was elected to the United States House of Representatives for the First District in 1912 and reelected consistently to the House through 1920.

The Caraways resided in progressively nicer homes in town. Around the time of his election to Congress, they owned a dignified two-story house downtown at the corner of Warner and Madison in the best area of Jonesboro. It is no longer standing. The Caraways attended the Methodist Church. Thad was a member of the Elks and Knights of Pythias.

Hattie was a popular friend and neighbor who was invited to be a member of Jonesboro's prestigious Twentieth Century Club, a ladies' group in which she was voted secretary. Some of Jonesboro's senior citizens recall their mothers revealing that during World War I, the club decided to forego sweets at their meetings in favor of more austere offerings. One day when Hattie was hosting, she passed a bakery with a display of chocolate confections in the window. Unable to resist, she bought them for the club despite its self-imposed austerity. The treats were swiftly consumed with no sanctions against her.

When Thad was elected to Congress, a move to Washington was necessary. Hattie was forced to write the Twentieth Century Club this letter, signing it "'Resigned' Secretary:"

> *It is with great reluctance that I submit my resignation as Sec. of this most Honorable Club. My mistakes—almost sins of omission—have been*

Hattie Wyatt Caraway as a young wife in
Jonesboro, circa 1904. *Courtesy Caraway family.*

*condoned by the President who has been so wonderful in many ways—and
my regret at leaving you all I cannot possibly express—However, I shall
be returning—and the fact that I am to retain my membership, with that I
shall have a definite place among you when I return takes away much of
the sting of my transplanting. Wishing everything good to every member,
individual and collectively, and all good things for the club always.*

Hattie with her sons, Paul and Forrest (in her lap), circa 1910. *Courtesy Caraway family.*

Hattie with Forrest (left) and Paul, circa 1914. *Courtesy Caraway family.*

That was the extent of her world and elective experience at the time, one to which she had all intentions of returning.

COOKING, SEWING, VOTING

Hattie was able to vote for her husband in the U.S. Senate race of 1920, the first year American women were allowed to vote. Was she a fiery advocate of women's suffrage? Did this ignite her interest in politics? Apparently not. In 1937, she told a journalist that she simply added voting to cooking, sewing and other household duties.

Above: Caraway family portrait (Thad at right, Paul at left, Forrest second from right, Robert in lap), Washington, circa 1916. *Courtesy Caraway family.*

Left: Congressman Thad Caraway. *Courtesy Caraway family.*

Along with her husband, Hattie had three sons to take care of. Her first-born, who would become Lieutenant General Paul Wyatt Caraway (1905–1985), and her middle child, who became Brigadier General Forrest Caraway (1909–1985), were both born in Jonesboro (and ironically, both died the same year.) Her youngest, Robert Easley Caraway, called "Bobbie" (1915–1934), was born after the move to Washington.

In 1926, Senator Thad Caraway bought the Calvert Mansion in Riverdale Park, Maryland, a massive five-part historical property whose construction dated to 1801 for the family of Lord Baltimore. This was the grand estate whose mortgage Hattie inherited after Thad's death and could not afford. Few people could. This was the residence that Huey Long used to such advantage during the 1932 campaign without mentioning that it was a mansion: "While she was there in the Senate, a-standing by you, the sheriff sold her home for a mortgage she couldn't pay because she didn't have the money," said Long. "That was the test, my friends. With all the big-bellied politicians in Arkansas campaigning against this one little woman, she stood by you in spite of the fact that the sheriff was selling her home over her head."

The letters in the Kays archives show that college president V.C. Kays of Arkansas State University had first attempted to establish a working relationship with Thad. Though the college was in Jonesboro, the Caraways' hometown, Thad was not known for being its champion.

Hattie Caraway, however, had living reminders of her hometown all around her, even in the nation's capital. Far from distancing herself, she embraced them. Fannie Cash, who was one of the first African American employees at Arkansas State, joined Hattie's household in Washington as cook/housekeeper and stayed there until her passing. Hattie publicly acknowledged how indispensable Fannie Cash was in taking care of the household, allowing her to concentrate on work in the Senate. Mosie Wyatt Abbott, Caraway's sister who later worked at the Library of Congress, had taught courses in education at Arkansas State during the 1920s and was a living reminder of those back home.

Thad Caraway was polite though not overly helpful in at least one of his dealings with the college back home. The school's main building burned to the ground in 1931, a disaster for the new institution. This building was the school's lifeblood, housing its classrooms, administrative offices, science laboratories and library—in short, most of the school. Its loss was a catastrophe; only the charred student records in a safe were saved. Thad expressed sympathy, but his response to Kays on January 17, 1931, was perfunctory, even addressing it "Dear friend" rather than by name:

Senator Thad Caraway. *Courtesy Caraway family.*

I am tremendously disturbed of the loss of the Administration Building and your library and other valuable property. I hope you are adequately covered by insurance. If so, you will be all right. If not, I am afraid we are in for a hard time, aren't you?

*   *With best wishes, I am*
*   *Sincerely yours*
*   *T.H. Caraway*

Thad was reelected to the Senate in 1926 and planned to run again in 1932. But he died suddenly in a Little Rock hospital of a blood clot after surgery for a kidney stone on November 6, 1931. He died at age sixty, the same age of Hattie's father when she was born.

Thad's passing left a grief-stricken widow and a problem for Arkansas politicians.

THREE DAYS

If Thad had lived just three days longer, Arkansas governor Harvey Parnell could have simply appointed someone to fill the empty seat, even himself. But Arkansas law called for a special election, and the Democratic party needed immediate political balance in the Senate. A "seat-holder" was needed to fill the spot while the men prepared to run in the 1932 election. They decided to allow Thad's widow, Hattie, to have the honor and receive the senatorial salary she desperately needed after her husband's death.

It was not an unusual gesture in Arkansas. In 1929, Pearl Oldfield was allowed to fill out her husband William's term in the U.S. House of Representatives, and Effiegene Wingo, widow of Representative Otis Wingo, completed his term in 1930.

Nor was it unknown for a woman to have set foot in the U.S. Senate. Rebecca Latimer Felton, widow of a Georgia congressman, had that honor at age eighty-seven after being appointed as a reward for civic contributions in that state. She was sworn in and sat in the Senate for all of one day in 1922. Felton was even permitted to make a short speech, in which she predicted that other women would follow her into that august chamber, serving with integrity and usefulness.

So it was not without precedent to help a politician's widow in that way. Based on history, Hattie was, of course, expected to step aside when the "real candidates"—the men—were ready to run.

The most immediate report of the ensuing plan came within hours of Thad's being laid to rest. The *Jonesboro Evening Appeal* of November 10, 1931, was headlined "Widow Slated for Senate Seat":

> *With the announcement that she would accept the nomination of the state Democratic central committee to fill the unexpired term of her famous*

*husband if it is offered to her, it appeared practically certain here today that Mrs. Hattie Caraway would be the second woman ever to hold a seat in the United States Senate...**Although she made no statement regarding the matter, leaders were confident that Mrs. Caraway would not seek to succeed herself in the next general election*** [emphasis the author's].

SPECIAL ELECTION

On November 13, 1931, Governor Parnell made the interim appointment for Hattie to fill Thad's seat in Washington. On December 9, she was sworn in as a U.S. senator. It was at this time that she began keeping a journal, perhaps with some thought of publishing it in a women's magazine or possibly as a way of recording her thoughts that would have to remain unexpressed aloud.

It is interesting that almost fifty years later, an article in *National Business Woman* magazine styles her "in every sense of the term, a displaced homemaker, who at age 54, was forced by economic necessity to re-enter the labor market." The same article, written in 1979, also claimed Caraway as a member of the Business and Professional Women's Club of Jonesboro, though it is not stated when that might have been. In 1931, the Twentieth Century Club was Caraway's sole credit.

A special election was called for January 12, 1932. Governor Parnell put forward Hattie's name to hold the seat for the Democrats and finish out Thad's unexpired term, which would run through March 1933.

Little Rock attorney Frank Pace also sought the nomination, but his candidacy was opposed by those who felt his election would give him an unfair advantage if he ran for the full six-year term. That was the whole point of installing a safe seat-holder. Thad's former law partner in Jonesboro, Basil Baker, helped mobilize an organization for Hattie to counter Pace.

Though Sam Carson and Rex Floyd, who filed as Independents, also announced for the office, the only real obstacle in the special election was paying for it. After being challenged to support one of their own, the Arkansas Democratic Women's Club was formed to raise money and awareness of the election as well as recruit female volunteers as election officials. The club succeeded on all counts. For a cost of the $37.50 filing fee, Hattie Caraway won easily and made history.

She then concentrated on learning the requirements of her role in the Senate, though her journal proves she understood what the males of the Democratic hierarchy expected. They assumed they would "give" her the short-term seat as a widow's sufferance, maintaining the Democratic party's voting presence in the Senate. They also assumed that would be the end of it. Hattie Caraway could be a footnote to history, following the twenty-four-hour tenure of Rebecca Felton.

From contemporary newspaper reports in 1931, Hattie Caraway had made no public statement herself one way or the other. But leaders, all male, were said to be "confident" she would not run for the full term. How could it be otherwise?

Chapter 3

SEAT-HOLDER

1931–1932

"I guess they wanted as few contaminated as possible."

Hattie Wyatt Caraway won the special election as she was supposed to, and on January 12, 1932, became the first woman seated as an elected U.S. senator.

She was placed by herself on the back row of the Senate chamber and told by a staffer that she was given the same desk used by Rebecca Felton. Caraway confided to her journal, "I guess they wanted as few contaminated as possible."

Not neglecting her manners, personal or political, she wrote thank-you notes after the special election. On January 15, 1932, Hattie wrote this note to V.C. Kays. It contains themes that would often be seen in her letters: appreciation for others, desire to do as her late husband ("Dad") would have done, concern for people back home and self-deprecation.

I thank you very much for your telegram and the confidence expressed in my ability to play up satisfactorily for my constituency. This, of course, was made possible by your efforts and other friends who were enlisted and I want you to know that I sincerely appreciate it all. I think the people generally in Arkansas do not realize just how great is the favor shown me and how much needed. I realize more and more that I can not possibly do the things Dad did, but I must try to represent and reflect his feelings in matters. Of course, in many ways I have to make up my own mind and I will probably make a great many mistakes of judgment but it will not be because I am not

ASU founding president V.C. Kays and Senator Hattie Caraway.

trying to take into consideration the best interest of the people of my state.
I hope to come home before long and attend to some business and get the
matters of Dad's estate in some shape so that I will know where we are. In
the meantime, I am wishing for you all health and prosperity.

PERSONAL LITTLE JOURNAL

It was at this time that Caraway began writing a journal on Senate stationery.
It ran sporadically from December 14, 1931, through March 28, 1934, with a

huge gap between June 6, 1932, and January 3, 1934, which she recognized, writing, "Little journal I have neglected you." The earliest entries concentrate heavily on clothing and food, combining both in Caraway's second entry:

> *Dec. 15, 1931: Sen. Lewis is dressed in a tan shirt with green stripes, green tie, low cut vest of creame—looks like linen—Beige Spats. His shirt sleeves are very long, cuff buttons of enamel, black ground with red flowers...They're still discussing wild life and I'm getting very hungry. Think I shall introduce a bill for a regular luncheon hour, all Senators to be fired if they do not eat in that hour.*

Some of the food-related journal entries of early 1932 speak for themselves:

> *Feb. 8: Had lunch. Awful—soup and tomatoes—coffee 35¢, tip 10¢—making 45 cents. That's pretty bad.*
> *Feb. 18: Went to office, et [sic] a sandwich and cup of coffee (15 cts).*
> *Feb. 22: Pressed chicken, dressed eggs, whole ham, hot potato boats, peach preserves, hot biscuits and strawberry shortcake. Some spread for poor folks.*

Those are the type of things her critics cite as evidence of her ineptitude. Her earliest entries make it hard to argue the point. But by her final entries, Caraway has grown into an articulate, thoughtful and perceptive legislator, grappling with the issues of the day:

> *March 24, 1934: This journal continues to be neglected while we wrangle over patronage, St. Lawrence Waterway Treaty, Philippine Independence, liberally interspersed with cries from Robinson of Indiana that the President of the U.S. is a murderer. Air mail contract cancellation being the order for wholesale murder of Army Fliers...But of all the spectacles the attitude of the Senate in regard to Sen. Long's personal objections to D.D. Moore was one of the most indefensible...The chance to satisfy personal spleen puts the Senate in no admirable light.*

Though her early journal entries seem trivial and though in her own words she downplayed her abilities compared to her late husband, Hattie Caraway sincerely wanted to help people in those troubled times. They were not Depression-era statistics; they were her friends and neighbors back home. They had names and faces. She strived to help individuals, as well as obtaining programs for the state and buildings for its institutions. As a former schoolteacher, she also recognized that education was the road out of poverty.

As she entered the Senate, she was called, and was in many ways, a typical 1920s housewife. However, she was also a departure from the average woman of her time. She had more education than most, was well read, had worked outside the home as a teacher and had managed the family's small cotton plantation.

Moreover, she lived a great part of her life as the wife of a politician, including being part of Washington's social scene with her ambitious husband. Any gathering in the nation's capital revolved around politics; like the movie industry in Hollywood, it was a factory town. While Hattie may not have been socially prominent, she was intelligent enough to absorb and understand what she overheard.

She was not, however, exemplary in every way by today's standards. Her journal reveals that she reflected both small-town provincialism and the ingrained Southern mores of one born only a decade removed from the Civil War.

Caraway joined other Southern senators in voting against anti–poll tax and anti-lynching legislation, explaining her resistance as support for state's rights. In her second day as a senator, she wrote, "A Miss Silverman or Stein or something Jewish pushed into my office. I was terribly indignant. She got no interview." On January 9, 1932, she wrote, "Another letter from a fool in California. Nuts from where the nuts come from. What more could you expect."

In her new role, she could be both self-deprecating and then defensive of her gender. On December 22, 1931, she wrote: "I wish I knew how I was going to vote. One minute I'm for one side the next just the opposite. The arguments are not convincing—And I'm sorry I cannot make up what passes for my mind." However, it was followed soon after: "And they say women talk all the time. There's been a lot of 'old woman's talk' here tonight—but I haven't done any of it."

With the visual evidence of her status as an outsider in the last row, she was, for the most part, ignored by her fellow senators, though not by the American news media, which followed her every move, especially in matters of clothing. She was not unaware of being a media darling, writing at one point in her journal, "Today I almost made the front page as I lost the hem out of my petticoat."

Petticoats aside, Hattie Caraway did have a formidable weapon. It was Garrett Whiteside.

"NINETY-SEVENTH SENATOR"

John Garrett Whiteside (1885–1947) was well known and highly respected in the halls of the Capitol. He served as congressional secretary for many of the Arkansas delegation of U.S. representatives and senators during a career that spanned 1907 through 1947. In the era when there were ninety-six senators representing the forty-eight states, he was often called "the ninety-seventh Senator." In a twist of history, he was also instrumental in the declaration of both world wars.

Whiteside was a native of Nashville, Arkansas. As a young man, he served for a time as a court reporter, arriving in Washington, D.C., in 1907 as secretary to Representative Ben Cravens of Fort Smith. Whiteside remained at the Capitol in continuous service for four decades, subsequently becoming secretary to Representative Otis Wingo until 1921 and Senator Thad Caraway from 1921 until Thad's death in 1931. When Hattie Caraway succeeded her late husband, she and Whiteside agreed that he would remain as her congressional secretary.

Whiteside was recognized and respected in Washington. The *Congressional Record* of April 21, 1941, includes a tribute by Representative Fadjo Cravens of Fort Smith: "Quiet, retiring, unassuming, Garrett Whiteside probably knows and is known by more people in the Capitol and congressional offices than any other person. Those places have been his workshop for 34 years. There he has seen history made, and he has helped make it."

Garrett Whiteside. *Courtesy Whiteside family.*

Part of that history came when Whiteside was serving as congressional clerk for the Committee on Enrolled Bills in 1917. When Whiteside was asked if he knew how to use a typewriter, he said that he could, having served as a court reporter. Thus he typed the declaration of America's entry into World War I. Then, on December 8, 1941, Whiteside, again serving as clerk for the Committee on Enrolled Bills, delivered the declaration of war to the White House, signaling America's entry into World War II. President Franklin Roosevelt said, "It is remarkable that you should have handled both resolutions which commit this country to the greatest wars in history."

When Hattie took office, Garrett Whiteside acted as chief of staff, helping her to maneuver through the maze of the innumerable challenges she faced. Whiteside's presence was crucial to Caraway as she settled in. If she had harbored any hopes of being shown the ropes by her colleague, Arkansas' senior senator Joe T. Robinson, she was mistaken. He was civil to her, if nothing more, apparently waiting for Arkansas' next "real senator."

For Robinson, it was a rare miscalculation.

JOE T.

Attorney Joseph Taylor Robinson (1872–1937), originally from Lonoke, Arkansas, was an esteemed national figure when Hattie Caraway entered the Senate. He had pulled himself up by his bootstraps with less than four years' formal education to become a law school graduate and fearsome debater. In Arkansas, he served as state legislator and governor before being elected to the U.S. House of Representatives (1902–13) and the U.S. Senate (1913–37). He led successful legislative efforts that were considered both populist and progressive. He served as chairman of the Democratic National Convention as well as being the Democratic leader of the Senate as minority leader, then majority leader.

At the Democratic Convention of 1924, Robinson was one of several unsuccessful "favorite son" candidates for president. But in 1928, he was officially nominated for vice president, becoming the first Arkansan and first Southern Democrat since the Civil War to run on the national ticket. His Craighead County campaign co-chair was Thad Caraway.

Robinson campaigned by train across much of the nation, gaining admirers for his speaking ability as well as for being an outspoken opponent of the Ku Klux Klan and religious bigotry. Though he and his running mate, Al Smith, lost to Herbert Hoover, Robinson had become a national figure, embraced by many Republicans as well as conservative Democrats. When Franklin Roosevelt became president, Robinson pushed many New Deal programs through the Senate. He was a force to be reckoned with.

Because of his national status, many of Robinson's friends were equally esteemed figures. His law office in Arkansas represented some of the state's wealthiest businessmen. While he and Thad Caraway were cordial as Senate colleagues, it was said that they did not move in the same circles. That certainly extended to Hattie.

Robinson had purchased the magnificent Foster house on Broadway in Little Rock, described as the most prestigious house in Little Rock's most prestigious neighborhood. Even today, the stately Victorian stands proudly near the Arkansas Governor's Mansion. When Thad Caraway bought the massive Calvert Mansion in Maryland, did he have Robinson's house in mind?

Scholar Diane Kincaid notes some of her sources speculating that if Robinson had been more cordial to Hattie Caraway, she might not have been as drawn to Huey Long. One of Caraway's journal entries hinting at their distance came on January 4, 1932, soon after she entered the Senate: "Sen. Robinson came around only for a moment at the instigation of Mr. Biffle."

Leslie Biffle of Piggott was Robinson's highly respected assistant and Democratic party secretary. He was as politically astute as Hattie's own Garrett Whiteside. While Robinson's law firm did represent the kind of forces she and Long would later refer to as "Wall Street" rather than a populist viewpoint, the two Arkansas senators could have been supportive colleagues. Instead, if it appeared that Robinson was pushed to be minimally civil to her only at the urging of his assistant, she may have felt personally snubbed. Already alone and vulnerable, she would not have appreciated Robinson's perceived noblesse oblige.

SENATORESS

On January 13, 1932, Hattie modestly noted a history-making moment in her journal by simply listing election results as she became the first woman elected to the United State Senate, following the tally arriving from back home in Arkansas. "Everyone was most kind," she wrote.

The following day, her newfound place in history caused some chafing with the astute Whiteside, who no doubt recognized the political currency in positive press: "Almost a run-in with Garrett—because he wants to let me in for too much publicity."

Presumably, they reached a compromise. Caraway must have known what a valuable asset Whiteside was to have in her corner; Whiteside understood publicity.

When America's most popular celebrity, Will Rogers, visited Washington on February 10, 1932, and was introduced to Caraway, newsmen captured the moment. She was delighted with the photos the next day, including one autographed to her by the humorist. It was inscribed, "To my friend the Senatoress. Will Rogers."

While some say Garrett Whiteside was the "real" senator, others dispute that allegation—including Whiteside himself, who said he was "amazed" by Caraway's grasp of the issues. There is absolutely no doubt that he ran her office with skill and efficiency, even as Hattie brought homey touches. She was in her office every day and at her desk by 8:00 a.m. She usually brought her own lunch. Sometimes she brought sandwiches and homemade candies for her staff. *TIME* magazine noted that outside her door "in the mahogany-&-marble Senate Office Building stood a little row of milk bottles." Each morning, she diligently read the previous day's *Congressional Record* and studied upcoming legislation.

Whiteside managed it all with intelligence, grace, political savvy and an apparent good nature, well liked and highly respected at the Capitol. His wife, Pearl, became a good friend to Hattie Caraway; the Whitesides often dined with the senator. Garrett Whiteside's importance to Hattie cannot be overstated. Soon afterward, the same might be said for a Louisiana Kingfish.

Sign from Senator Caraway's office door. *Courtesy Caraway family.*

Enter the Kingfish

Colorful, controversial Huey Pierce Long (1893–1935) enjoyed calling himself the "Kingfish," taken from the popular *Amos 'n' Andy* radio program of the day. He was called other things too, including demagogue and dictator.

He hailed from Winnfield, Louisiana, in the northern part of that state. He spent his early years as a traveling salesman, often visiting neighboring Arkansas. He entered state politics, ultimately serving as governor of Louisiana from 1928 to 1932 and as U.S. senator from 1932 to 1935. He espoused a program that he called "Share the Wealth," with a motto and even a theme song called "Every Man a King." The concept gained more and more appeal to destitute Americans as the Depression tightened its grip.

As a Democrat, Long backed FDR in the 1932 election but was infuriated when Roosevelt failed to back his Share the Wealth plan. Many say it was at that point when Long began seriously considering challenging Roosevelt in the 1936 presidential election, or at least in 1940 when most expected FDR to leave office.

Long ran successfully for U.S. senator in 1930 while still serving as Louisiana governor. Assured then of being a player on the national stage, he remained in the governor's office until early 1932. He had postponed his departure for Washington in order to keep a finger on things at home and out of spite for his lieutenant governor. Long admittedly loved the limelight and hoped to expand its glow beyond Louisiana to the rest of the nation. The means to do so would come from an unlikely source.

When Huey Long finally arrived in the Senate, his flamboyant ways led him to be treated as an outsider. He was seated accordingly, next to the lone woman, Hattie Caraway. They struck up a tenuous friendship.

Actually, their paths had already crossed. When Thad Caraway attended the Cotton Conference at New Orleans in August, 1931, Hattie accompanied her husband. Thad was a polite supporter of many of Long's ideas to aid cotton planters. Since Thad had held a favorable attitude toward Huey Long, Hattie did so as well.

Her first journal entry concerning Long was on December 17, 1931. It reflects her clear understanding of his personal and political style, as well as a degree of affection for his having shown deference to her late husband: "Have just learned that Huey Long is to have seat immediately to my left. I'm wondering if he won't have some trouble taking his seat. I'm also wondering who will escort him to take the oath. He had asked Dad to do that. He will bring color and quite a display of fireworks I imagine."

Long officially entered the Senate on January 25, 1932, but ironically, Caraway missed the moment: "Company kept me so long I missed seeing Sen. Long take the oath. I'm sorry." A further irony was that Long was escorted by Joe T. Robinson, whom the Kingfish would later attack viciously for not supporting his Share the Wealth plan.

The next day, Hattie appreciated the consummate performer in action: "Mr. Long arose, addressed the chair in a loud voice...He has good voice and perfect stage presence."

REFUSED TO PROMISE

In light of later allegations, Kincaid notes a significant incident on January 25, 1932, in which Caraway is brought a copy of an article about her in the January 24 *New York Times* by R.L. Duffus, entitled, "A Woman Treads New Paths as Senator."

Kincaid says it is one of the few articles that pleased Hattie. In it, Duffus stated she was asked to agree not to run for the full six-year term, but "this promise she refused to give." Duffus was a noted reporter who later served on the *Times'* editorial board. He was probably not easily fooled nor inclined to puffery. He says that though she listened in the Senate instead of talking, "she exerts an influence in committee through her votes."

February 1, 1932, was a noteworthy date for Caraway. She gives equal weight in her journal to it being her fifty-fourth birthday, to her home (the Calvert Mansion) selling, to her Senate credentials arriving, to being sworn in as a U.S. senator and to receiving an award from the popular Evening in Paris perfume for being the first woman elected to the Senate.

The nature of the Evening in Paris prize has been lost to history. "It is really very lovely," she notes in her February 4 journal entry. "I feel badly to accept so handsome a gift."

Lost in the shuffle was Thad, or so it appeared to the outside world. However, even with the accolades, it is important to remember that Hattie was still the grieving widow of a recently deceased husband, as reflected in her journal entry for February 5, 1932: "My 30th Wedding Anniversary. And Dad has been gone nearly 3 months. No one will ever know how much we miss him."

The downside of national fame was brought close to home in February 1932, as newspapers including the *New York Times* ran the embarrassing story of her brother's arrest. Walter "Dick" Wyatt was arrested in Tennessee on charges of violating the Volstead Act, or Prohibition, by operating a still, to which he pleaded not guilty. On February 18, Hattie wrote, "First thing that stared me in the face was the news story that my brother was caught in a dry net. If he was guilty, I'm glad they caught him. If innocent I hope he can prove it."

Though her brother was later acquitted, it must have been mortifying for Hattie to see her name linked in print to a miscreant brother since she herself was so strongly against alcohol. She opposed the repeal of Prohibition, a legislative stance that was held against her in later years as archaic.

The journal entry for February 25, 1932, was doubly significant. First, she affectionately noted the return to the Senate of Long, familiarly calling him by his first name as he apparently livened up her day: "Huey in much perfection sartorially came back. Asked how his pardner was and whether she was true to the Kingfish." Then there was an interaction with Robinson that brought forth a noted Caraway line: "Guess I said too much or too little. Never know."

By February 29, 1932, Caraway was looking to the political future. Far from being indifferent to the upcoming race for her Senate seat, she was considering what course to take, sizing up the potential competition in her journal while also expressing her own self-doubt: "Every day it is more borne in on my consciousness that to try to fill Dad's shoes is a rather large undertaking…I can well know that they are easier on my feet than they'd be on Parnell's or Kirby's. Dear, dear, I wish I could know what is the course to pursue. None of us can look into the future tho. The way I figure Kirby's backing will be good, but not too popular. He has slipped into the Senate once over a dead man's body." William Kirby of Texarkana had served out the term of Arkansas senator James Clarke who, in 1916, died in office; Kirby was then defeated in the general election by Thad Caraway. It is uncertain if Hattie noticed the irony in her statement.

Significantly, she goes on: "Parnell can not claim any promise from me for none of his efforts to buy me succeeded. **I refused to make any promises**" *[emphasis the author's]*.

She made a trip home to Jonesboro at this time and enjoyed seeing old friends. Upon her return to Washington, on March 10, 1932, she made a point of noting, "Joe has not come to speak to me." Perhaps she felt slightly less alone in her perceptions after a conversation with a senator the next day who said that many fellow senators "are so pompous—and that Joe is both pompous and mean." She immediately caught herself: "This is a pretty personal little journal, but I will edit before it's published—if ever. Doesn't it sound big to think or talk of having something published?"

Like many women before and after, it must have been a comfort to have her "little journal" in which to confide, in the absence of female friends or mentors. After seeing squabbling among certain senators and feeling they could have reached conciliation through simple civility, she would certainly not admonish them but wrote, "Oh well, a woman on suffrance here may only think, and put in a private journal any thoughts she may have."

SOUL-SEARCHING

As noted earlier, she often voted with a kind of homespun wisdom, but significantly, she also learned to note the larger implications, including those to the economy. On March 14, 1932, regarding the Senate proposal from dairy-producing states to ban butter substitutes from federal agencies, including St. Elizabeth's Hospital for the Insane in Washington, Caraway wrote, "I feel that crazy people have as much right to butter as sane ones, so I voted for butter instead of oleo. Funny. I couldn't feel as if it were of national importance. Maybe I had not thought enough of the cotton seed products...Had luncheon with Sen. Long. He voted with me on this—hope it wasn't wrong for that reason. Sen. Logan says he voted aye too because I did—whew—of course my vote counts."

She had a realistic, amused view of Long and his very real liabilities. On March 16, 1932, she felt confident enough in her new friend to facetiously ask Huey to autograph a copy of a virulently anti-Long biography, *Tin Pot Napoleon*, noting succinctly, "He did not."

The next few months revealed a good deal of soul-searching on her part regarding whether to run for the full term. It also marked the escalation of Long's attacks on Joe Robinson, which put her in an awkward position, literally and figuratively. One day she wrote, "Huey got up and read an editorial in the Post of some days ago. He made a perfectly mad speech. Being right next to him I had to sit thru it. My eardrums suffered."

On March 24, 1932, she received the editor of the *Jonesboro Sun* newspaper who came to visit: "He wanted to know, as a friend, if I were to be a candidate. I was non committal."

Through April of 1932, Long continued to step up his assault on Robinson. Along with his anger that Robinson refused to support some of Huey's proposals, there may have been a degree of jealousy over Robinson's national prestige and power as Senate leader. The Kingfish loved the spotlight, and there was not room in this one for both. He even invaded Joe's territory. On April 13, Caraway noted, "Huey sat in Joe's seat nearly all day. Neeley says Joe will do well if Huey lets him stay in Senate another term. That he is the most eager person to burst into limelight on all occasions of anyone he ever saw. He's right on every count—but didn't ask me to concur."

Soon Long would invade Robinson's territory in a far more literal—and momentous—way.

Chapter 4

CANDIDATE

1932

"I shall have a wonderful time running for office whether I get there or not."

May 2, 1932, might have been an interesting day to be a "fly on the wall" as Hattie Caraway met Jeannette Rankin. In 1916, Jeannette Pickering Rankin (1880–1973), a Republican from Montana, was the first woman elected to Congress. This was four years before American women were given the right to vote. Rankin was a blunt, outspoken crusader for issues including women's rights, child welfare, civil rights and, especially, pacifism. She had been one of fifty in the U.S. House of Representatives to vote against America's entry into World War I in 1917, but it was she who was singled out and pilloried by the press. After some time out of office, Rankin was returned to Congress in 1941, just in time for the vote on America entering World War II. Again, she voted against war, this time the only member of either the House or Senate to do so. Again, she was vilified. It was said that she escaped into a phone booth and cried. Still going strong in 1968, Rankin was an activist against the Vietnam War, leading marchers to protest in Washington.

On the day of their meeting in 1932, Caraway wrote, "Miss Rankin, 1ˢᵗ woman Congressman came in. I'm not strong for her. Not any sort of jealousy the cause either. I do not like her manner. I do not like her reputation, etc." Caraway does not elaborate on the specific cause of her disdain, but suffice to say they did not become best friends. In any case, Caraway had other things on her mind.

THE PLUNGE

As the May 10 deadline approached to file for the 1932 Arkansas primary, Caraway's journal reflected her thought process at the time. She pointedly referred to her conflicted feelings as well as her dread of what might happen when she left office, of being dependent on others. After she made her decision, the announcement was buried and almost anti-climactic. Strained aquatic metaphors ensued:

May 3: Guess my political life is nearly over, as well as my physical one. It saddens one to think of the years and years of dependence one may have to endure.

May 6: After Monday, I'll either be much keyed up or on my way back to the simple life, maybe.

May 9: Made history. Presided over the Senate…It was snap judgment and I was scared. Nothing came up but oh, the autographs I signed. Well, I pitched a coin and heads came three times, so because the boys wish and because I really want to try out my own theory of a woman running for office I let my check and pledges be filed. And now won't be able to sleep or eat.

May 10: After much indigestion and little sleep I am still gasping for breath after jumping off the "deep end." The water seems very chilly and I can not swim a single stroke. However, I can dig in and kick and keep afloat—and by pushing with my toes I often make it across the pool. If possible, I shall strangle and choke and cross this pool, with my courage intact—and come up still loving human kind regardless of the outcome. I will not deny that I would sleep better and enjoy my food more if I had not plunged.

May 11: Thank God (in all reverence) that I am able to eat and sleep and laugh at myself. If I can hold on to my sense of humor and a modicum of dignity I shall have had a wonderful time running for office, whether I get there or not.

STAMPEDE

She had announced her shocking intention to run for a full six-year term on May 9 when she was presiding over the Senate by request of Vice President Charles Curtis. It was one day before the filing deadline.

The next day, Caraway posted the required fees for the August 1932 Democratic primary, which in Arkansas at the time all but guaranteed election. After her surprising decision to run, no one gave her much chance of winning. She was lost in a six-man stampede.

Some speculated that Governor Parnell himself would run for the Senate seat, but he was beleaguered by events at home. His stand on private relief efforts ran counter to the ebullient presidential candidate, Franklin Delano Roosevelt of New York, who clearly caught the mood of the nation in 1932.

The field for Arkansas' Senate seat narrowed to six. In alphabetical order, they were:

- Osee Lee ("O.L.") Bodenhamer of El Dorado, a businessman who had been national commander of the American Legion
- Charles Brough, former governor and economics lecturer at the University of Arkansas in Fayetteville
- William George ("Big Bill") Hutton, popular former Pulaski County sheriff
- William Fosgate Kirby, associate justice of the Arkansas Supreme Court and the former U.S. senator who lost reelection to Thad Caraway in 1920
- Melbourne Martin, a Little Rock attorney with family political ties and money for extensive advertising
- Vincent Miles, who had served on the Democratic National Committee for almost two decades

Kirby characterized his opponents as "three majors, a widow, an irresponsible ex-governor and an ex-sheriff." Individually, they each had strengths. Some claimed close ties to FDR (who endorsed none of them). Most had state or national credentials. All felt they had what it took to be Arkansas' next senator.

None reckoned on the Kingfish.

PLACE IN THE SUN

After her decision to file, Caraway sent out letters to gauge support but did not get much in the way of assurance, which did not escape her notice. On May 13, she wrote, "The mails are really too stingy of approbation or objection to my announcement. However, the die is cast—and all I can do is sit tight and take whatever of abuse or praise comes from such a blow to tradition. Really the way of the Politician is hard."

The announcement of her candidacy, while groundbreaking in itself, took a back seat to the fireworks on the Senate floor. Huey Long had escalated his attacks on Joe T. Robinson, and others now began to echo Long's assaults on Robinson's ties to powerful, wealthy businessmen, whom Long called the "money interests."

Robinson gave as good as he got. Once, he played to the Senate galleries in a broadside directed at the Kingfish who, Robinson noted, was so fond of quoting "scripture." Robinson cited what he felt was a particularly apt verse for Long from Job 8:2—"How long shall the words of thy mouth be like a strong wind?"

While Robinson was not close to Caraway, she felt compassion for her Arkansas colleague. Her journal of May 18 read, "I'm sorry Joe has fallen on evil days. He really is so attractive when he unbends." But on the very next day, he inspired her to write, "I very foolishly tried to talk to Joe today. Never again. He was cooler than a fresh cucumber and sourer than a pickled one."

It was while Caraway was in that frame of mind after Robinson's rebuff that a historic move was made, followed immediately by Caraway's depth of concern. She knew the Kingfish and "the way of the Politician." On May 21, she wrote, "Huey called me, offered to donate to my campaign and work for me. I can't sell my soul and live with myself. It would mean nothing for me to sit here day after day and have no freedom of voting."

Still, nothing much happened. Her campaign progressed at a glacial speed. Caraway finally left Washington to begin campaigning in mid-July, with less than a month to go before the August 8 primary.

Her train stopped in Memphis, where she made a statement to the press that seemed to stem from a previously unseen rebellious spirit: "Again, let me deny these rumors that I will withdraw from the race. I never said a word that would indicate withdrawal…I am going to fight for my place in the sun. The time has passed when a woman is placed in a position and kept there only while someone else is being groomed for the job."

A major problem was that most Arkansas politicos and experienced campaign staffers were already pledged to other candidates. Arriving in Jonesboro, she discovered that even influential hometown friends were pledged elsewhere.

She left for Hot Springs, where she chose young attorney Marshall Purvis to be her campaign manager, though he was untested, having no real experience in that arena.

"Might Go, If Asked"

Huey Long tantalized the press with vague intimations that he "might go, if asked" to campaign for Caraway in her home state. He returned to New Orleans, fired up his organization and, on July 19, announced his intention to help Caraway in neighboring Arkansas. He said he did so over the objections of his political machine.

Author David Malone quoted Long as saying, "I got hold of our gang down there [New Orleans] and I told them I wanted to raise some money to help Mrs. Caraway. They looked at me and said, 'Huey, you're crazy, it can't be done...' I told them, 'Let's take a vote. I'm the chairman, I vote Aye, and the motion is carried. Now get out there and raise some money.' And they did."

Printed handouts such as "Wall Street vs. the People" headed for Arkansas by truck. In one, Caraway's name was misspelled, but Huey's intent was clear:

Dear Friend:

I am doing what I can to offset the outside financial influence that is being exerted against Senator (Mrs.) Hattie W. Carraway. All over this country the senators who are standing by the people are marked for destruction by the big financial masters of Wall Street. Mrs. Carraway is one of the marked ones.

One of the saddest things that can ever happen to the people of this country, under present conditions, is to have those few persons who are standing by them to be defeated for re-election.

We are now nip and tuck in the Senate. The fight is on. It is a fight for the people on one side and for their serfdom on the other side. We are trying to hold what votes we have and gain a few more; because there has got to be a change made for the common people of this country.

I am herewith enclosing you some documents, issued by me and by the American Federation of Labor in defense of Mrs. Carraway. Our interest is only for the people. Will you please hand these out to your neighbors and friends after reading the same. If you need more, write to me and they will be sent you, just as many as you can use, even if it be a few hundred.

In the name of the people whose battle we are trying to wage, I will personally thank you for this.

Your friend,

Huey P. Long

The stage was set; the show was about to begin. But what made Hattie run and Long support her?

SURPRISED, ASTONISHED, SHOCKED

The responses to both questions are neither simple nor clear-cut. Why did Hattie defy traditional barriers and run for the Senate? Her granddaughter, Mrs. Hill, is not sure of all the detailed circumstances surrounding her grandmother's history-making 1932 campaign and election. But she did hear that Hattie's eldest son, Paul, a West Point graduate, three-star general and alumnus of Georgetown Law School, at least partially helped convince Hattie to run for reelection. "I don't know for sure about her wanting to run," said Mrs. Hill. "Maybe it was a little of both of them."

Certainly her female Arkansas predecessors appointed to the House of Representatives offered no clue. Kincaid said, "Hattie Caraway never made any such explicit public disclaimer herself, but had there been any doubts of her intentions, other factors would have resolved them. Two wives of deceased Arkansas congressmen had recently taken seats in the House of Representatives under similar circumstances, and neither Pearl Oldfield nor Effiegene Wingo attempted to extend her tenure in office…I interviewed many men, all of whom said they were surprised, astonished, shocked when Sen. Caraway announced she would seek election to a full term. A female friend of Sen. Caraway's said that she was not. 'But virtually all of the politicians I've talked to were dumbfounded,' I pointed out. 'Of course,' she replied. 'They are all men.'"

Kincaid stated that while some of Caraway's supporters may have done so on her behalf, Hattie herself neither made nor authorized any commitment, adding that Caraway's son Paul specifically recollected her silence: "I can still see her in the rocking-chair in the front room as all the politicians came to call. She rocked and rocked, but she didn't say anything."

Immediately after her husband's death, Hattie was probably too shell-shocked to say anything, much less make long-term plans. Later she had time to think and to observe her surroundings in the Senate. Additionally, a great part of the answer may lie in her May 3 journal entry, exactly a week before the filing deadline: "It saddens one to think of the years and years of dependence one may have to endure."

Dependence. Her husband was gone, and her sons were West Pointers with military careers. Without an income, would she have to live with one of them on an army base, possibly with a young family, or rotate among them year after year, again "a woman on 'sufferance'"? After being in the center of power, where each day brought excitement and meaningful work, could that be traded for…well, not very much?

ADVENTURE

The options for a widow of modest means were limited. It is possible she could have been appointed postmaster someday back home in Jonesboro. It was a job she did, in fact, acquire for a widowed friend, Mrs. Floy Parr. Perhaps she could have found a job of some sort in Washington, maybe at the Library of Congress like her sister Mosie Abbott, or even a civil service position, which she would later obtain after leaving the Senate.

Or…run for a full term. Why not give it a try? She had certainly observed enough in the Senate to think she had a mind as good as anyone there. She was extremely effective in the committee setting, where most of the Senate's work was done. She served on the Agriculture Committee, one of the Senate's most important in the 1930s when the economic upheaval of the Great Depression and the disastrous Dust Bowl drought threw the nation's food supply into chaos. She knew firsthand about issues such as flood control and farm policy, more than the "manicured men" of the Senate. She responded to every request for help that came to her office. She sincerely had the welfare of people in Arkansas at heart. She stayed awake at her Senate desk. She had Garrett Whiteside. And, as she wrote the day after she filed, if she could hold on to her dignity and sense of humor, it would be wonderful running for office, whether she won or not.

If she lost, it would not really be the end of the world. Why not run?

It would be an adventure.

Why, then, did Huey Long offer to help? Many sources reduce Long's motivation to simple self-interest. In keeping Caraway as a senator, he might gain a rubber stamp for his pet programs. That was no doubt one of the possibilities. Along with that, however, there was more likely a complex mix of the political and the personal by a complex man.

First, he was locked in a power struggle with Arkansas' other senator, Joe T. Robinson. Though Caraway required that Long not attack Robinson in her campaign, there would be many delightful opportunities for innuendo at Robinson's expense.

By going into Arkansas, Long had the chance to expand his influence outside his home state of Louisiana. He could test the national waters for a possible challenge to Franklin Roosevelt in the 1936 presidential campaign. He could speak at great length, right to the people, give them his handbills and get his ideas out.

If his star power helped get Caraway elected, something generally considered impossible, he would emerge as a political miracle worker of unchallenged strength.

Championing a lost cause, centered around a woman no less, would generate excitement and publicity. It would guarantee visibility and voracious coverage by news media across the country. He and his ideas would be in the spotlight. And the Kingfish did love the spotlight.

It is also probable that Huey genuinely liked Caraway. He had gotten along with her late husband. As seatmates, he and Hattie were cordial, while many senators snubbed him. As Southerners, populists and Democrats, they truly had a lot in common politically. Biographers also note that Long could appear sentimental at times, even chivalrous. In this case, rescuing a tiny Southern widow would have been in keeping with that side of his complicated nature.

And if she lost, it would not really be his fault, would it? But if she won…!

It would be an adventure.

Speaking Announcements

Senator Hattie D. Caraway

———— and ————

Huey P. Long

U. S. Senator (former Governor) of Louisiana

MONDAY, AUGUST 1st, 1932

MAGNOLIA	9:00 A. M.	Court House
EL DORADO	11:00 A. M.	Court House
CAMDEN	2:30 P. M.	Court House
FORDYCE	4:30 P. M.	Political Park
PINE BLUFF	8:00 P. M.	Mo. Pacific Park

TUESDAY, AUGUST 2nd, 1932

STRUTTGART	9:00 A. M.	East of Court House
BRINKLEY	11:00 A. M.	City Park
FORREST CITY	1:30 P. M.	Court House
WYNNE	3:00 P. M.	Railroad Park
HARRISONBURG	5:00 P. M.	Court House
JONESBORO	8:00 P. M.	Court House

WEDNESDAY, AUGUST 3rd, 1932

WALNUT RIDGE	9:00 A. M.	Band Stand
NEWPORT	11:30 A. M.	Remmel Park
BATESVILLE	2:30 P. M.	Fair Grounds
SEARCY	4:30 P. M.	Court House
LITTLE ROCK	9:00 P. M.	Band Shell

THURSDAY, AUGUST 4th, 1932

RUSSELLVILLE	11:00 A. M.	Court House
BOONEVILLE	3:00 P. M.	Court House
FT. SMITH	8:00 P. M.	Andrews' Field

FRIDAY, AUGUST 5th, 1932

MENA	11:00 A. M.	City Park
MT. IDA	3:00 P. M.	Court House
HOT SPRINGS	9:00 P. M.	Whittington Park

SATURDAY, AUGUST 6th, 1932

MALVERN	9:00 A. M.	Court House
ARKADELPHIA	11:00 A. M.	Next to Library
PRESCOTT	2:00 P. M.	Court House
HOPE	4:00 P.M.	Municipal Auditorium
TEXARKANA	8:00 P. M.	Court House Lawn

Original speaking schedule for 1932 campaign tour. Hattie Caraway Collection, University of Arkansas. *Photo by David Huff, Bob's Studio of Fayetteville.*

Roaring into Arkansas

So, on August 1, 1932, Huey Long roared into Arkansas. He had spent time in the state as a salesman early in his career and so was no stranger to the state, as some opponents alleged. He managed to work anecdotes of his previous Arkansas visits into his campaign speeches, of which it was said none were written down and no two were exactly alike.

Caraway and Long's whirlwind sweep of Arkansas in August 1932 has been documented in the Malone book as well as being portrayed onstage in the play, *Miz Caraway and the Kingfish*. It was a grueling campaign, with few paved roads to travel on as they barnstormed the state. Caraway suffered from stomach upset, and Huey needed throat spray for this voice. They spoke in more than thirty town squares, climbing up on top of their vehicle to speak where it was often so hot that their shoes galvanized to the roof of the truck.

The original campaign tour for Caraway and Long was amended many times, but as they set out, they followed the speaking schedule on the previous page.

In the Backseat

Their speeches were generally held at courthouse squares, local parks or fairgrounds. As the campaign with its intriguing new sound trucks rolled through the state, more towns clamored for them to appear. New locations were added, and Long extended his Arkansas visit by several days to accommodate them. Most estimates place the final total at thirty-nine appearances over eight to nine days. Fascinated Arkansans stood by the roadside to see the campaign caravan as it raced past.

Even with today's paved roads, safe cars, interstate highways, air-conditioned vehicles and convenient motels, it is a grueling schedule. By the end of the hot, dusty tour, the fifty-four-year-old Caraway, the lone woman among Long and his men, had elicited his respect for her capability and endurance. She in turn had improved her public speaking by learning from the Kingfish himself, master of the art.

The 1932 pro forma Arkansas general election in November would place Hattie Caraway firmly in her history-making seat in the U.S. Senate. Even before November, however, contemporary writers were spotlighting one of the most colorful campaigns in American political history.

Arkansans, like this group outside Jonesboro, stood by the roadside to see the campaign caravan pass.

The October 15, 1932 issue of the weekly *Saturday Evening Post* featured a five-page article by noted writer Hermann Deutsch. Deutsch was uniquely qualified to cover the Caraway/Long campaign. He was a daily commentator on Long's special brand of politics, which allowed him insight into what was called the "Louisiana Medicine Show" that invaded Arkansas. Deutsch held a doctorate from the University of Chicago and wrote for the Chicago *Journal* before moving to New Orleans.

There he served from 1949 to 1970 as a daily columnist, associate editor and chief editorial writer. Along with four decades covering Louisiana politics every day for the *States-Item*, he was a contributor to top national magazines including *Collier's, Esquire* and the *Saturday Evening Post.*

Deutsch was along for the ride on the August 1932 campaign trail. In fact, he sat in the backseat of Huey's car with Hattie. She originally had her own car, but after once being late to a campaign appearance when she visited too long with supporters at the previous stop, Huey had her ride in his car with him. He slept in the front seat while Hattie sat in back with Deutsch and occasionally other newsmen.

Barely two months had passed when Deutsch's article "Hattie and Huey" appeared in the popular *Saturday Evening Post*. Along with its iconic Norman Rockwell covers, the magazine published top writers such as William

Faulkner and Scott Fitzgerald, averaging about three million readers each week in the 1930s. Therefore, the Deutsch article guaranteed Caraway name recognition far beyond the borders of Arkansas, and an incandescent national spotlight for Long for his role in the campaign.

Deutsch's article is a fascinating eyewitness account of the 1932 campaign from a trained observer in the middle of the action. He did not waste time before stating his perception of the spectacle, calling it "bizarre," and saying, "On August 1, 1932, Hattie W. Caraway of Jonesboro, Arkansas, was merely a senator's widow. Huey P. Long of New Orleans was merely an eccentric political dictator in Louisiana…By suppertime of Tuesday, August ninth, Mrs. Caraway was the first woman ever nominated—which means elected, in Arkansas—to a full six-year term in the Senate, after a real fight…Huey P. Long had also, in effect, served notice on the members of the Senate of the United States…that those who crossed the Kingfish did so at their political peril."

QUICK STUDY

Deutsch cited the "entry of modern, high-pressure technic into still another field…direct personal contact with thirty-nine crowded mass meetings in as many county seats scattered over an entire state along 2,103 measured miles of highway in the space of seven short days and nights. That sort of thing demands organization, which…the Kingfish ain't got nothing else but."

Grammar notwithstanding, Deutsch recognized that Long was bringing a new kind of political campaign to the fray.

Perhaps as a result of one of their backseat chats, it is Deutsch who stated that "Hatty" was the original spelling of Caraway's first name. And it is Deutsch who cited Long's animosity toward Arkansas' senior senator Joe T. Robinson as a motivating factor in his Arkansas incursion. Deutsch also stated that Caraway's support of Long's resolution to limit individual incomes to $1,000,000 convinced the Kingfish that her vote in the Senate was "important to the common people."

With tongue firmly in cheek, Deutsch also painted Long as a sentimentalist: "Six of those big politicians back in Arkansas campaigning against one lone, little, defenseless woman while she was working in Washington for the people—and against Joe Robinson! Monstrous!"

For all the nation to see, the Deutsch article described the Caraway campaign caravan, its innovative use of sound trucks, handbills and what today would be called advancemen who dashed ahead to the next stop, drumming up the crowds. He even cites incidents of Long's "wide-shouldered young men" quieting babies whose vocal chords competed with the Kingfish.

It was Deutsch who quoted Huey as telling Caraway not to worry about the campaigning: "We can make that campaign in one week. That's all we need. That won't give 'em a chance to get over their surprise."

And the campaign did surprise the people of Arkansas. Even today, the logistics are masterful. According to Deutsch, the campaign caravan consisted of seven trucks, plus Long's private car. "Two of the trucks were the specially designed and built sound trucks developed by him for his Louisiana forays. Each is equipped with four amplifying horns…On the roof of each truck is a slatted platform…with nested take-down iron railing and a portable stairway."

Deutsch cited Long's fiery public speaking, finally bringing Caraway into the picture by applauding her as a quick study who developed amazingly in a week. He said that in the beginning, her preliminary remarks could not even properly be called a speech. "Two days later she was an effective stump speaker in her own right…Incidentally, she did not need much tutoring, for she possesses a happy gift for phrase making."

CIRCUS HITCHED TO TORNADO

Long was quoted by Deutsch as exhorting the crowd on the gender issue, tying it to the Wall Street interests. "If you turn your hand against this woman senator who stood by you, you'll never be able to get anyone from this state to stand by you again," he quoted Long, who continued, "Oh, they tell you they don't want a woman in the Senate, but that ain't it, my friends. They don't want *this* woman. If she had voted with them, they would have had her picture on the front page in the press and on the magazine covers as that great woman statesman from Arkansas."

It was a dazzling campaign conducted with military precision. One of Huey's drivers recalled tearing over gravel roads between stops at seventy to eighty miles per hour, blowing six sets of tires that week as they careened at death-defying speeds.

This was the campaign that spawned the expression that has been used to describe the carnival-like atmosphere of Arkansas politics in general.

Variously attributed to a reporter, a political observer and an opponent, it was widely quoted that the campaign moved through the state "like a circus hitched to a tornado."

Hattie Caraway won that election with more total votes than all six men who ran against her put together. While there are those who say she would not have won without Huey's help, she also defeated her opponents in thirty-two counties where she and Long did not campaign. In doing so, Hattie Caraway was elected to a higher government office than any other American woman to date.

Her colleague and fellow Arkansas senator Joe T. Robinson had publicly maintained neutrality in the 1932 race.

The following year, in 1933, *Every Man A King*, subtitled "The Autobiography of Huey Long," was published. In the book, Long's only take on the spectacular Caraway campaign was brief, devoid of introspection and focused on just one issue:

> *...I campaigned in the State of Arkansas for the election of Mrs. Hattie W. Caraway to the United States Senate. She could never forget nor cease to laugh over the plans we made for caring for obstreperous infants in the audience so that their mothers might listen to the speeches without the crowd being disturbed. I remember when I saw her notice one of our campaigners take charge of the first baby. The child began fretting and then began to cry. One of the young men accompanying us immediately gave it a drink of water. The child quieted for a bit, and resumed a whimper, whereupon the same campaign worker handed the baby an all-day sucker, which it immediately grasped and soon fell asleep. Mrs. Caraway did not understand that it was a matter of design until it had been repeated a number of times. I left Mrs. Caraway at Jonesboro, Arkansas, on Monday evening, taking a train at Memphis at midnight for my home in New Orleans. The election occurred the next day. Over the radio early in the next night I learned that she had received more votes than the combined vote of all her opponents.*

That was Huey's uncharacteristically brief take on the historic campaign in its entirety, focusing solely on squalling tots.

Historian Stuart Towns summarized the 1932 campaign as "a Louisiana Medicine Show." In his opinion, "there is little question but what the Kingfish with his emotional appeals to the Depression-stricken farmer and businessman; his tried-and-proven political style; his caravan of sound trucks (the first ever used in an Arkansas political campaign), campaign literature and circus-like advancemen, was directly responsible for Mrs. Caraway's return to Washington."

Marian Baker Thielman of Jonesboro was a college student when Huey's caravan rolled into town. Apart from being an eyewitness to history, she had more than a passing interest. Her father, Basil Baker, had been a law partner of Thad Caraway and helped mobilize Hattie's first campaign. In 2004, Mrs. Thielman recalled, "This was the first time our town saw a car going around asking for votes and playing music. My father said that she did not need him [Long], that the name Caraway was so popular that a yellow dog could have won if he was named Caraway and no one would know the difference."

Whatever the reason(s) for the outcome, whatever the incentive(s) for Caraway to run and whatever the motive(s) of Huey Long in supporting her, Hattie Caraway of Arkansas was the first duly elected full-term female United States senator.

Now the work would begin, at one of the worst possible times.

Chapter 5

SENATOR

1932–1938

"My idea of this job is to do my best in all matters where I can be of service."

In 1932, America was struggling through the depths of the Great Depression. It was reflected in one of the top tunes of the year, the grim anthem "Brother, Can You Spare a Dime?" Charles Lindbergh's baby was kidnapped, with tragic results. The Bonus Army marched on Washington, which also did not end well. People were losing farms that had been in their families for generations. It was a bleak time of desperation when many reasonable people predicted a revolution in the United States. In the 1930s, some Americans feared that the hard times might be here to stay.

Yet in 1932, there were also bright spots. The buoyant Franklin Delano Roosevelt was elected president. Amelia Earhart was the first woman to fly the Atlantic solo. And Hattie Caraway of Arkansas was the first woman elected to the U.S. Senate.

Bright spots were desperately needed. The Depression continued its death grip on the country, made immeasurably worse by the dust storms devastating America's plains. But FDR knew the power of hope, and Hattie Caraway set out to help those who needed it.

Less than six months after the 1932 election, a *Ladies' Home Journal* article called her a good Southern wife "in the best traditional sense" and praised her stamina and courage. Yet the next paragraph referred to her sitting "huddled during sessions apparently absorbed in crossword puzzles" and says her "first official utterance was 'The windows need washing,'" something

People back home were losing their farms, such as this 1930s farm family near Jonesboro.

that would follow her for years. The 1945 edition of *Current Biography* repeats it, adding that it was her first official utterance on entering the Senate. The U.S. Senate Chamber has no windows.

THE MAZE

In April 1933, Hattie Caraway was significant enough to rate a mention in the *New York Times* and other publications for having been bitten at a White House reception by the Roosevelts' German police dog. Since the dog also tried to bite British Prime Minster Ramsay MacDonald, at least she was in good company.

Along with mentions in the national press such as that, her famous name was also linked to punch lines in items such as one in the Syracuse (New York) *Journal* published February 1, 1934, ironically on her birthday. A column called "Stars and Stripes," which had no byline, included small, would-be humorous bits used as filler on a slow news day. Below the blurb

"By pushing with my toes, I often make it across the pool." *Courtesy Caraway family.*

"What is this thing called spring?" came: "Senator Hattie Caraway believes in women's rights and privileges; she demands the right to enter the Senate cloakroom where senators cuss and smoke but asserts her privilege to stay outside and not cuss and smoke."

In the Senate, she was finding her way through the bureaucratic maze. One day she took out her journal for the last time. The March 28, 1934 entry was the final one. It is noteworthy in that the journal had progressed significantly from the heavily clothes-and-food-centered minutiae of the early entries to more substantive thought.

Additionally, while she was almost always a strong supporter of FDR, she was not a blind follower. In this entry, she expressed her distaste for the way he asked for her vote on an issue that was important to him, not in friendship but with a threat: "Here on March 28 1934 I want to inscribe in this journal the account of the only time the Pres. has talked to me in the interest of any measure that was at all close in the Senate. The St. Lawrence Waterway Treaty. He called me up the evening before the vote was taken—and instead of asking me as a personal favor or for the good of the country to vote for the treaty he made a covert threat to veto a little personal bill namely to exempt Little Rock College from the payment of $1,400 loss to war department for materials destroyed while the College was given over to the use of the ROTC."

She also found herself in a poor position on matters of patronage for political positions back home against Arkansas' senior senator Joe T. Robinson. No doubt she felt she had at least as many favors to repay as Robinson and apparently was at this time not asking for much. After speaking on the matter with FDR confidant James Farley, she noted that "he was most friendly to my desire to name at least one friend to a place of importance." Realistically, though, she questioned how much Farley could help.

A similar appeal on the same patronage matter with U.S. Attorney General Homer Cummings was less satisfying: "He was nice—sympathetic—but insisted that Joe and I get together. That is always to give him his own way." Hattie was no fool when it came to dealing with powerful men.

An added comment by Cummings struck a sour note with Caraway: "The one thing that broke my heart in that interview was the Attorney General suggested that should my man fail to get the place that I at least am 'having the fun of being the Senator.' If there is any fun in being a Senator I've yet to find it. My idea of this job is to do my level best to represent the people of my State, not only in matters of legislation but in all matters where I can be of service. Enough of this. These are all things everyone meets face to face in this job, but we are supposed to count it all fun because we are elected to high office."

CATCH-22

Back in Jonesboro, V.C. Kays brought overwhelming Depression-era problems to Caraway, which he requested that she resolve immediately, such as his letter of April 6, 1934: "We are getting a good many requests here at the college at the present time from people who are on direct relief or work relief and who want to get government loans to…start farming and to make a living at home while working in industrial labor. I do not know what to tell them…I shall appreciate it very much if you will let me have this information by return mail."

She continued her work for education all across Arkansas. In July 1934, the Reconstruction Finance Corporation reported back to Caraway regarding interest rate reductions on self-liquidating loans for projects including those at Henderson State Teachers College in Arkadelphia and the Agricultural and Mechanical College at Monticello.

Some pleas for Caraway's help were heartbreakingly personal. A typical letter, on April 18, 1934, involved people who found themselves in a Catch-22 situation:

Dear Senator Caraway:

I am living at the present time in Luster Township in Craighead County. I am a brick layer by trade and have made my living as a brick layer for thirty-two years. I have been working in and near Jonesboro for some eighteen years. I have a wife and seven children. Three of the children are sick in bed now. I could not pay rent in town so I built a log cabin in the woods. Now I am told I am not eligible for work relief because I live outside the city. All I want is a chance to work and I have to have that to make a living for my family or my family will have to go on relief. I will certainly be indebted to you if you can help me get some work.

In the midst of national despair, Hattie suffered a devastating personal loss. Her youngest son, Robert, called "Bobbie," was killed at age nineteen on August 1, 1934. He died after being thrown from a horse while visiting his cousins and Aunt Ludie Wyatt Jones at Newbern, Tennessee.

The event was significant enough to be noted in the *New York Times* as well as other national newspapers. His funeral was held at Jonesboro's First Methodist Church on August 4. Senator Caraway was offered a final resting place for her son, who had been on leave from West Point, at Arlington National Cemetery outside Washington. However, she preferred him to be interred at Jonesboro's Oaklawn Cemetery next to her late husband, Thad.

More sudden death would follow.

DEATH OF A KINGFISH

In September 1934, Caraway sent a handwritten letter to Kays. It contained touching personal themes. First, she had helped a young person go to college: "Mary Sue's mother said they were all so happy because I had spoken to you, and she was jubilant because she could be in school." Of course there was work: "We still find plenty to do, and lots of people to see." She missed her son Paul, who was away in the army; was heartbroken over the previous month's death of her youngest son; and still mourned her husband, Thad: "It is good for me to have things to occupy my mind, now that Bobbie and Paul are both gone. Of course, Paul is only away and we can communicate with him. I'm trying to feel that Bobbie and his Dad are just away on a trip together, and are thinking of us but can't find time to write. Vain imaginings, but it helps over the worst spots." And finally, of course: "Tell Mrs. Kays that I'm not eating so much now and having less indigestion."

A brief and much less personal note from Kays passed hers in the mail: "Enclosed is a copy of a proposed bill for refinancing the public school indebtedness in Arkansas."

As the Depression persisted, FDR continued trying to spark hope and recovery in America with his New Deal. In 1935, he called for farm assistance, better housing, fair taxation and a radical proposal called social security. These were the issues before Congress when shocking news arrived from Louisiana.

Caraway's Senate seatmate and helpful friend Huey Long was dead.

Huey had been surrounded by armed guards as he walked the halls of the Louisiana State Capitol in Baton Rouge for a special session on September 8, 1935. He was approached by a young doctor, who, some witnesses said, punched Long. Gunfire then erupted in the narrow marble corridor. When the smoke cleared, the doctor lay dead and Huey was mortally wounded, dying two days later at age forty-two.

His memorial attracted a crowd estimated at more than two hundred thousand. Afterward, Long was buried on the grounds of the Louisiana State Capitol. His widow, Rose McConnell Long, was appointed to his seat in the U.S. Senate and was later elected to the position, making her the second woman elected to the Senate—after Hattie Caraway. It was the first time two women served in the Senate at the same time.

As she had stopped writing in her journal the year before, we do not know Hattie's immediate personal thoughts of Long's death. But in 1941, when a statue of Long was dedicated at the U.S. Capitol, it was Hattie who spoke:

> *Early in our careers in the Senate, Huey Long and I became fast friends. He sat near me. We often discussed the merits of those humanitarian issues in which we were both interested. While I did not always agree with Senator Long, I respected his judgment and his sincerity of purpose...This friendship ripened as time went on and never lessened until the day of his death. He was a loyal friend. No one knows that fact better than I do. In the rapidly moving field of politics, I came up for re-election. Senator Long volunteered his aid in my campaign. His desire to aid was sincere and without ulterior motive. He had little to gain if I were successful. He had much to lose if I failed. Let me say, to the credit of Senator Long, that he never sought to take legislative or political advantage of his assistance to me in that campaign. To the contrary, when it so happened that I disagreed with him, he showed*

*no displeasure, but praised me for doing that which I thought was right. He
at all times showed me every courtesy and consideration.*

Hattie, too, was a loyal friend.

Sought After

On October 18, 1935, Hattie traveled to Russellville, Arkansas, to attend
the dedication of a new women's dormitory named in her honor. Caraway
Hall at today's Arkansas Tech University in Russellville is still in use, was
renovated in 2005 and is on the National Registry of Historical Buildings.
A dormitory at ASU in Jonesboro, built thanks to Hattie's efforts, was also
named Caraway Hall; it opened in 1933 but was demolished in 1988. At the
time of this writing, no other buildings or markers honoring Caraway for
her contributions to ASU appear on that campus.

The letters below show Caraway doing her part with the Department of War
to establish an ROTC unit at Arkansas State. It would become a highly successful
program that produced a large number of army generals and was mandatory for
male students there until 1971. On December 11, 1935, she wrote to Kays: "I
have taken up personally with the War Department the matter of the ROTC Unit
and am doing what I can to be of some assistance. There was some little objection,
but I am trying to work it out. You may rest assured I will do everything I can in
this matter." Then, the following month: "It was with considerable pleasure that
I wired you yesterday that I had secured an ROTC Unit for the College. We had
quite a battle in this matter and are pleased that we were successful."

In February 1936, Caraway chaired hearings on industrial pollution of the
nation's streams, from which many people in rural areas drew their drinking
water. While some of her comments were sadly self-deprecating ("My
questions may seem kind of foolish…"), others were sharp: "[Businesses]
want to be left alone, but they are eager for [government] help."

June of 1936 saw Arkansas celebrating the Centennial of its statehood.
Caraway participated in the planning of this milestone, along with requesting
federal funds to help offset expenses for the Depression-stricken state. She
hoped the celebration would lift people's spirits during the hard times.

In the *State College News* of June 28, 1936, under the headline "Lady Senator
Speaks for FDR," it is noted that at this time, Caraway was in demand to
make campaign speeches for other candidates.

The *Piggott (Ark.) Banner* of January 1, 1937, was already speculating on the front page whether Caraway herself would run for reelection in the 1938 election. The item goes on to note the many factors in her favor, such as her influence among other members of the Senate, her increased self-confidence, national visibility by speaking in several states for candidates in the 1936 campaign and broadcasters who said she had "one of the most pleasing feminine speaking voices on the air."

Significantly, it added that she turned down many offers to write syndicated articles, to lecture and to become the "spokesman for feminist movements."

On March 3, 1937, an item ran in the *State College News* under the headline, "Mrs. Caraway Refuses Use of Her Name," which reiterated the fact that she was sought after:

> *Senator Hattie W. Caraway...has refused the offer made by a tobacco company agent to allow the use of her name in cigarette advertising. "I do not mean to criticize any one else," Senator Caraway stated, "but it seems to me that commercial endorsements are not in keeping with the dignity of the office we hold." This is not the only offer of this nature that Senator Caraway has turned down. Many are the advertisers who have hoped to capitalize on her advertising value as the only woman in the United States Senate.*

Caraway did not disapprove of smoking; in fact, she made references in her journal to enjoying a cigarette with friends. She simply took the dignity of her office seriously.

She would certainly never even have considered being part of a liquor ad even after the repeal of Prohibition in 1933. She was strictly "dry" and quite vocal about her anti-alcohol beliefs. When she was on the campaign trail with Huey Long in 1932, two things she recalled that he always carried in the glove compartment of his car were his Bible and what she referred to as his "gargles." Some have speculated as to their nature. It is unknown if Hattie saw the pistol that rested next to them.

It is interesting that the press reported she had been approached by a number of advertisers hoping to capitalize on her fame. Far from being insignificant or an embarrassment, she was known and courted. She was also in demand as a speaker, a far cry from the early days of her 1932 campaign when her radio addresses were described by her own campaign manager as "sweet little talks which didn't help and didn't hurt but did keep her busy."

Her family was also being noted in the national press by the late 1930s. Newspapers ran the story of her son Paul, with his infantry regiment in

Senator Hattie Wyatt Caraway. *Courtesy U.S. Senate Historical Office.*

China, being among the Americans in harm's way in July 1937 when the Japanese invaded Tientsin.

HOLDS HER TONGUE

In 1937, Caraway was again the subject of a lengthy article in a major national magazine. *Collier's* on September 18, 1937, ran "The Woman Who Holds her Tongue" by George Creel, bylined as the magazine's Washington Staff Writer. Like Deutsch in 1932, Creel was at the time a noteworthy writer.

He had worked as a reporter before starting his own newspaper, the *Kansas City Independent*, and had seen something of the world. In 1917, President

Woodrow Wilson appointed him head of the United States Committee on Public Information. There he organized public speakers in support of World War I and encouraged artists to create paintings, posters and cartoons promoting the war. He ran for California governor in 1934 and later accepted a WPA post from Franklin Roosevelt.

His article in *Collier's* began, "Slowly and somewhat painfully, Mrs. Hattie Caraway, Senator from Arkansas, has emerged, finally winning acceptance by male colleagues as a human being in her own right, amply endowed with brains and good, hard common sense, and actually possessed of a mind, courage and conviction."

The piece described how she originally filled her Senate seat and touched on 1932, when Huey Long came forward as her champion. Creel noted it appeared to some as a trade-off: the whirlwind Arkansas campaign in return for her Senate vote, with some seeing her as a bewildered woman who would be "Huey's echo."

Creel challenged that perception by quoting Caraway herself: "'Mr. Long,' I said, looking him squarely in the eye, 'I wouldn't give a dime for my seat in the Senate if I couldn't vote according to my convictions and my conscience.'" Several instances of her voting against Long are cited, and when asked by the journalist if Huey became angry, Caraway said, "Not at all. Just grinned, flipped his hand, and said oke or something like that. Yes, indeed…there was a lot in Huey Long you couldn't help liking. He may have needed spanking sometimes, but under his flamboyancy were some mighty fine, generous, human qualities."

It is in this 1937 Creel article that we find the much-referenced quote signifying Caraway's lack of interest in either feminism or politics: "Not that I was against women getting the vote…After equal suffrage, I just added voting to cooking and sewing and other household duties.'"

Creel took this opportunity to paint a verbal picture of Caraway in 1937 that has remained through the years: "Even without her own confession of domestic tastes, Mrs. Caraway would stand convicted on the strength of her looks: graying hair parted in the middle and drawn back into a simple knot; a figure that scientific diet has never cabined, cribbed or confined; comfortable, roomy clothes and a sense of complete capabilities, joined to an air of invincible placidity."

He concluded by stating that she looked as if she might start shelling peas at any moment. But he then granted that talking with her was a fine way to spend one's time. On the whole, it was a positive piece. A year later, she would need all the help she could get.

Chapter 6

INCUMBENT

1938

"I shall be grateful for any assistance which you may render me."

In 1937, another unexpected death rocked the Senate. Caraway's fellow Arkansas senator Joe T. Robinson died suddenly of a heart attack. With his passing, Hattie Caraway became Arkansas' senior senator.

She was joined in the Senate by Congressman John E. Miller (1888–1981), who was endorsed for the position by Caraway. Miller won a special election to fill the seat.

Caraway continued quietly working the people of Arkansas. Since her 1932 election, she had been praised in the press for her service to her home state and the nation. Her special efforts in agriculture, veterans' affairs, labor relations and especially education were lauded. "It was largely though her efforts that the building programs of various state institutions were initiated and consummated," said one.

Early in 1938, she accepted a bid in Jonesboro that might be the answer to a future trivia question as to whether Hattie Caraway belonged to a sorority. The *Arkansas State College Herald* of March 9, 1938, announced that she was inducted as an honorary member of the college's chapter of Alpha Tau Zeta, the first person to be so honored. The article, stating she was "well pleased," quoted Caraway as saying, "When I went to school, sororities were practically unknown. Now you have given me a great thrill. I feel that all I have missed was the 'rush.'"

Around this time, Caraway also served as a speaker for Jonesboro's Chautauqua Literary and Scientific Circle. On one occasion, the press

People back home were not statistics; they had names and faces, such as this group near the Caraway home in downtown Jonesboro.

reported that she spoke about her experiences in Washington as a senator, adding that she displayed "as always" a keen sense of humor, relating a series of incidents that she observed in the Senate. What those might have been are lost to posterity.

WRITE SENATOR CARAWAY

After some speculation in the press about her intentions, Caraway decided to run for the Senate again in 1938. Along with frequent candidate J. Rosser Venable, described primarily as a World War I veteran, her opponent was the formidable U.S. Congressman John L. McClellan (1896–1977). He had been elected to the U.S. House of Representatives in 1934 and again in 1936, serving there until his run for the Senate in 1938. Hattie Caraway faced a tough battle in the primary.

McClellan's unsubtle campaign slogan was, "Arkansas needs another man in the Senate." McClellan then seemed to contradict himself when, after criticizing Caraway for not making grand public speeches on the floor of the Senate, he said in a campaign ad that most important Senate business got done in Congressional cloakroom caucuses. His point appeared to be that the real work was done, as he put it, "man to man." Caraway excelled in the small group setting of committee work, person to person.

McClellan is also quoted in newspapers of the day with the chicken-or-egg contention that "the United States senate (*sic*), as long as it is constituted almost entirely of men, is not such an office as may be filled by a Woman (*sic*)."

While she did not have Huey Long to work his magic this time, Caraway did have an ally in Homer Adkins, Arkansas' collector of internal revenue. Adkins was a powerful politician who wielded control of federal patronage in the state and had political ambitions of his own.

One Caraway campaign piece should be a reasonably accurate representation of her efforts, as it would have been challenged by her opponent if it was not. It would seem to confirm her diligent work as a senator, offering specifics of her efforts in agriculture, forestry, flood control, committee work, excellent attendance record, labor issues, education, the National Youth Administration, Civilian Conservation Corps, Public Works Administration projects, employment, veterans' affairs and, especially, service to the state: "There is not a member of the Senate more ready to help her constituents than is Senator Caraway. No service is too small, and none too large, but that she will not give her best efforts to aid. She receives

Caraway supported veterans, the aged and disabled, such as this Depression-era group in the Andrews family grocery, Jonesboro.

as much, if not more correspondence, than any member of the Senate. It is a well known saying in Arkansas: 'Write Senator Caraway. She will help you, if she can.'"

All Work Together

Caraway felt the friction and pressure of the 1938 campaign, especially financially, as she referred in a letter to Kays regarding Homer Adkins's plan for a women's division. She proffered the quaint concept of not spending more money than she had:

> *Homer wants to take 4 rooms on the mezzanine at the McGehee Hotel (for women) and one extra for me personally. I feel that the extra expense would be prohibitive. I think we should only have one headquarters—no special woman's divisions either in Little Rock or in counties—Let all work together—There are so many factions in both the women's and men's organizations, and I feel there'd be less friction and less wear & tear on me. I am not going to assume any indebtedness to be paid later. If I lost I couldn't pay—and if I won I would feel I was working for honor only should I assume a lot of debt. A race can be run that will fit the funds, I think.*

For someone as conscientious in attendance as Caraway, she was nonplussed that her opponent spent so much time at home campaigning and away from doing the people's work in Congress. She wondered whose side the newspapers were on. In a letter from Washington on June 11, 1938, she said, "I have just received information that McClellan is having 3 sound trucks brought in and is mapping out his itinerary and is getting his speeches ready. Maybe I will be home by the time he gets started. It seems rather surprising to me that he has been home and away from work here for 10 days with no mention of it in the papers. It may be that they feel it would be giving him too much publicity, or it may be that it is an act of friendship to him that they do not call the attention of the people to the fact that he has left his job here to attend to his own selfish desires."

Rolling with Roosevelt

On June 23, one day prior to the event, a postcard was mailed to Craighead County residents inviting them to what was called a Caraway Homecoming Celebration in Jonesboro "in honor of Senator Hattie W. Caraway, Arkansas' most distinguished citizen, as a tribute of respect and affection for the excellent service she has rendered her people." It featured a ladies' luncheon, reception, parade with five bands, speeches, band concert and a "Bathing Beauty Revue, after which will come a Mammoth Fireworks Display."

Bathing beauties aside, it was a nice tribute to a local celebrity who did not forget folks back home, as well as boosting visibility and goodwill toward her 1938 reelection campaign. Soon after, this campaign letter with her signature was sent to Arkansans who had sought help from Caraway's office:

I am writing this letter to the thousands of those in the state to whom I have tried to be of assistance since I have been a member of the United States Senate. My files show I have tried to be of assistance to you. While I am not asking that you support me in my race for re-election because of this fact, yet I do trust that you will feel kindly toward my campaign and I shall be grateful for any assistance which you may render me...

The June 28 *Log Cabin Democrat* in Conway praised Hattie's help in Central Arkansas by securing funds for road construction, a hospital annex, a new high school and the new Faulkner County courthouse.

During the summer of 1938, Hattie Caraway was not the only one campaigning. Though it was not a presidential election year, Franklin Roosevelt boarded a train to shore up support for the New Deal across the South. As leader of the Democratic Party, he planned to boost the candidacy of those favorable to his administration.

On July 9, Roosevelt's train paused briefly in Little Rock to allow Senators Hattie Caraway and John Miller to board. At 10:00 a.m., their train pulled into Booneville, its only Arkansas stop. The gathering has been estimated at everything from three hundred to three thousand people.

FDR emerged from his air-conditioned railcar into the steamy cauldron of an Arkansas summer. He listened as Caraway briefly introduced him and then gave the crowd what it had been waiting for: the magic of FDR himself.

In his comments, Roosevelt stated that he had known Caraway for a quarter of a century, calling her "a very, very old friend of mine and a friend of yours." Though she was an ardent supporter of the New Deal in the vast majority of issues, that was the extent of his endorsement. Historian Susan Dunn says that the White House believed she only had a fifty-fifty chance of reelection, and the president was being very cautious. However, he had no words at all for Caraway's opponent, John McClellan.

Since Thad Caraway was first elected to the U.S. House of Representatives in 1912, Roosevelt had no doubt crossed paths with Hattie in the previous quarter century, as he said. And since FDR offered no support at all to McClellan, even small praise for Hattie was better than none.

PREJUDICE AGAINST WOMEN

During the campaign, V.C. Kays wrote to Caraway that "there is still a certain amount of prejudice against a woman Senator." To help counter this, he advised her to be specific about her achievements. Then, on July 23, 1938, he sent out two-page letters to alumni of his school.

He linked Caraway's efforts with the Reconstruction Finance Corporation and the Public Works Administration, which brought about the construction of new buildings at Arkansas State College. He also highlighted Caraway's role as a pioneer in federal aid to education.

His statement that Arkansas schools would begin receiving $50,000 to $60,000 in federal funds for the first time due to her work becomes more dramatic when we consider that the entire 1932 budget appropriation from the State of Arkansas for his school was only $94,000. Federal funds, through Caraway's efforts, would mean a huge increase in the operating budget, availability of scholarships and work-study assistance.

In his letter, he also touched on her work for levees and drainage districts, much needed in the flood-prone state:

> ...*Senator Hattie W. Caraway secured for Arkansas State College the first Federal loan ever made to a college or other division of a State. She then helped the other colleges and the University to secure some three or four million dollars for their improvements.*
>
> ...*She is one Senator who has demonstrated her interest in her people and especially in the education of the youth of the State. She was the first member of the Senate and the first member of Congress to publicly endorse Federal aid to education.*

HATTIE W. CARAWAY
United States Senator

Caraway 1938 campaign poster.

...You also know of the excellent services which she has rendered in the securing of funds for levees, refunding of drainage districts, etc. I do not have time or space to enumerate the many things she has done for Arkansas. I hope that you will be active in her behalf; and that you will see that your friends, relatives, and neighbors assist in every way to send her back to the Senate and continue the exceptional service which she has rendered to the people of your state.

"OUR SENATOR"

On July 23, 1938, a news report in the *Fayetteville Daily Democrat* confirmed Caraway's general policy of not attacking her opponents but merely stating her record. This she did in a campaign visit to Fayetteville, which attracted thousands to the square.

She generously credited former Senate colleague Joe T. Robinson for his part in federal road funding even though he had passed away the year before. And she repaid FDR's support earlier in the month by endorsing him and, by extension, his still-controversial New Deal, though she denied being merely a rubber stamp for his programs.

Speaking at length about her federal school legislation, a subject meaningful to the well-educated Fayetteville community, the newspaper said she claimed more than 1,500 school buildings had been built in the United States as a direct result of her efforts for education.

Caraway stated that she had been helpful in the construction of new buildings for the University of Arkansas, the state's flagship land-grant institution, located in Fayetteville. If this had not been true, she no doubt would have been shouted down by the well-informed local crowd, many of whom were employed at the university. Buildings constructed at the U of A with federal funding in 1935–37 alone include the University Library (today's Vol Walker Hall), Gibson Hall, the Chemistry Building and men's gymnasium. If she had exaggerated her help to the U of A and then been jeered, it would no doubt have been reported.

An editorial in the same newspaper was simply titled "Our Senator." While unsigned, it was probably written by its astute publisher, Roberta Fulbright. Mrs. Fulbright was a formidable person and the mother of soon-to-be president of the University of Arkansas, her son Bill.

Mrs. Fulbright was a Caraway supporter who might well have endorsed Caraway's bid for the Senate again in 1944. But Caraway's opponent in that future race would be the one person Fulbright could not turn her back on: that same son Bill.

In 1938, however, Caraway had a friend who wrote:

> She has demonstrated her ability to serve on equal terms with her colleagues. An entire outsider, a corporation lawyer from Washington, in fact, a man not given to awarding women any place save in the home, had this to say: "I met with the Senate committee on Agriculture and Sen. Caraway knew better what she desired for her constituents and why she desired it than any other member."...That proved to me what I already believed, that she really holds her place, discharges her duty wisely and conscientiously at all times, and is as capable as those with whom she serves...She's a person, one to be proud of, one to support, one of the famous women of the world.

While still not directly attacking her opponent, there was one issue that brought forth Caraway's ire on the campaign trail. Having her own exemplary record of attendance in both the Senate chamber and in committee meetings, she examined McClellan's record in the House of Representatives. She found it unconscionable and shared the findings that of eighteen bills the House considered in 1937–38, McClellan was absent when fifteen were up for a vote.

World-Famous Stateswoman

Caraway's campaign staff created this flyer based on the letters of her name. It was not only a visually effective campaign piece, but underscored what many contemporaries saw as her strengths:

HEAD, HEART AND HAND DEVOTED TO SERVICE
ALERT FOR THE WELFARE OF THE AGED
TRAINED IN SENATORIAL PROCEDURE
TESTED BY EXPERIENCE; TACTFUL AND TRUE
INDIVIDUALISTIC, INTELLIGENT, INDUSTRIOUS
EARNEST, ENERGETIC AND EFFICIENT

WATCHFUL OF ARKANSAS' INTEREST

CAPABLE, COURAGEOUS AND CONSTRUCTIVE
AGGRESSIVE FOR LABOR AND VETERANS
RELIABLE, RESPONSIVE AND REPRESENTATIVE
ACTIVE IN AGRICULTURAL ADJUSTMENT
WAR'S ENEMY THROUGH PREPAREDNESS
ARKANSAS' WORLD-FAMOUS STATESWOMAN
YOUR FRIEND AND MINE

These qualifications entitle Sen. Hattie W. Caraway your support for re-election on August 9.

Note that in 1938, Caraway sensed that war was coming to the United States and advocated preparedness, even as notable Americans of the time advocated isolation. Caraway, having both sons in the army, supported readiness as the best deterrent.

Caraway won the 1938 primary by a little over 51 percent of the vote. It was probably not as wide a margin as she might have wished, but it was a win nonetheless. She was back in office.

After this defeat by Caraway, John McClellan was ultimately elected to the Senate in 1942. But in the 1938 race, Hattie Caraway edged him out to become the first woman reelected to the U.S. Senate.

She did so without the pyrotechnics of the Kingfish. She ran on her record of quiet, hard work. She had earned her success, and the state reelected her. But any post-election euphoria did not last long.

Chapter 7

PUBLIC SERVANT

1938–1944

"I have been swamped with letters."

After she won her 1938 reelection, Caraway could at least take a break from campaigning. But she continued fielding pleas for help, such as this letter of December 7, 1938. The "Aggie" is a local term for Arkansas State University, which had begun as an agricultural school. The WPA is the federal Works Progress Administration office in Jonesboro, where a clerk helpfully suggested contacting Caraway:

> *Mrs. Hattie W. Caraway*
> *Dear Madam—*
> *I was in the WPA office yesterday to see if we could get anything on relief. She said that we could not because we were able to work. Now, if we cannot get work or relief either, what are we to do? She told me to write you and see if you would help my husband get on at the Aggie. She said she believed you would. If you would only investigate our need, you would find it just like I have wrote it. Now Mrs. Caraway, we have one boy that is paralyzed, has been ever since last year. He has had epliseps [sic] fits for 18 years and is paralyzed now. I wish I could talk to you personal, but I can't.*

Caraway enlisted help from Kays at Arkansas State on the woman's behalf. But in another matter two weeks later, she had to gently remind him not to speak for her to desperate job-seekers: "I am in receipt of your letter regarding the post office at Knobel. I note your statement that my office has written that I will do all I can. I am sure there is some error about this because the filling of post office appointments is something over which a Senator has no control. I have been swamped with letters from various parts of the state about these appointments, and I have invariably written them what I just told you."

INFIGHTING

Hattie also had to juggle a complex political situation in Arkansas. Homer Adkins had aided Caraway's 1938 Senate campaign and aimed next to serve as governor. Adkins's adversary, no friend to Caraway, was Carl Bailey, who served as governor from 1937 to 1941 and was referred to in the article below as simply "the Governor of Arkansas."

There was friction among the factions regarding the naming of a judgeship, and Caraway was enmeshed in the political infighting. Dyess in Mississippi County was a federally sponsored resettlement colony for impoverished Arkansas farmers during the Depression. Warm Springs, Georgia, was FDR's "Little White House." Georgia was also home to Fort Benning, where Caraway's son Paul had been stationed.

Despite all the matters swirling around her, her 1938 election win and her superior status as Arkansas' senior senator, Caraway remained conscientious about not losing time away from the Senate, as seen in her letter to V.C. Kays on April 5, 1939:

> *I saw the statement in the* Gazette *that the Governor of Arkansas would be going to Warm Springs. I am glad that he has tried to tamper with the Dyess Colony for I think that will show the Administration just what he is. Miller nor I neither one are in favor of letting him name his judgeship. I have heard several times where he has tried to get a finger in the pie and has tried to use some of the men up here, but I don't think anything will come of it.*
>
> *Someone told me the other day that they thought the President would make the appointment in the next few days. I don't know whether he will or not, but I hope he does. I want the agony over. I am going to Georgia tomorrow and will be gone until Monday but I think the Senate is going to recess from tomorrow afternoon until Monday, so I will not lose any time.*

Two days later, Kays advised a third party to contact Caraway and helpfully gave her home address: "I am leaving for Washington tomorrow morning and will talk the matter over with Senator Caraway while I am there. If you haven't already given her a detailed statement of the situation, send it airmail to her home, 5248 Colorado N.W."

That same day, Kays wrote another letter, this time to the director of the Works Progress Administration in Little Rock. He used Caraway's workplace as his home-away-from-home: "I am leaving for Washington tomorrow morning. You can get me at Mrs. Caraway's office if you desire to write or call me."

CONFLICTS GLOBAL AND TRIVIAL

While dealing with domestic matters and the problems of people back home in Arkansas, Hattie Caraway did not turn her back on global events. Whether her views were influenced by her sons, both army officers, or by her inherent pragmatism, she stated in an address to the Daughters of the American Revolution on April 21, 1939, her belief in the need for military preparedness.

The country was still mired in the Depression, it was the eve of World War II and she was in the middle of a barely comprehensible political squabble swirling in Arkansas. Yet Caraway and her staff also had to deal with minutiae such as this complaint in May 1939. V.C. Kays had mentioned it to Garrett Whiteside, who responded:

> *Dear V.C.*
>
> *You said something at lunch about the visit of Mrs. M. I didn't exactly understand it except that she thought I was complaining about having too many visitors. I do not recall her being in the office but one time, and I thought she had a very enjoyable visit. I was as nice to her as I could be. I try to be nice to everyone and especially folks like Mrs. M. As I recall, though I am not certain about this, she came to our office after lunch and said that she was up before 10 o'clock, the time on our door. I presume I explained to her that we had to have office hours to enable us to get out the mail. I never complain at anyone coming to our office. The fact is, I do not recall much about it, and if you can give me the information, I will appreciate it.*

Kays responded, noting factions "among the women" as if there were no others, such as the Homer Adkins/Carl Bailey male power struggle: "Don't worry about the Mrs. M. matter. She did some talking in Little Rock and I got it just before I came up there. I think it will work out all right. It is just another of those cases where folks feel that without their aid the election would have gone wrong; and with the two or three factions among the women in Little Rock and the state, it is a job to keep the records straight from the standpoint of hand shaking and back slapping."

But they were wise to heed the situation. As former House Speaker Tip O'Neill famously declared, "All politics is local."

In 1939, Senator Hattie Caraway was noteworthy enough that her attendance at her son Forrest's July 2 wedding to Betty Meddis was covered by the national press.

Then it was back to work. A typical letter from a young lady asking Caraway's help arrived on July 23:

> Recently I was in district and state voice contests and then I was chosen to sing on Gov. Bailey's Arkansas Day program at the New York World's Fair. While in New York, I passed a Major Bowes audition...Mrs. Caraway, I paid ALL of my own expenses on this trip and unless I get a scholarship in voice, I will not get to go to school next year...Mrs. Caraway, I know you are a busy woman but will you please recommend to Arkansas State College that they give me a scholarship?

Caraway did. The girl was able to return to school on a work-study stipend, as did two sisters from Cherry Valley who were alone and penniless on their family farm after the death of their father. There is no way to know how many individual lives were touched in this way, how many young people for whom Caraway knew education was the way out of desperation.

CRITICAL MATTERS

Amid the pressures and pleas for help, Caraway's health was deteriorating. She was rushed to the hospital with a perforated ulcer, had emergency surgery on December 10, 1939, and remained in critical condition for some time. A perforated ulcer can be a serious medical problem in which the ulcer burns through the wall of the stomach, allowing stomach acid to escape into the body. Movie icon Rudolph Valentino had suffered a perforated ulcer and died at age thirty-one.

Caraway's condition was serious enough to be covered by the *New York Times* and other newspapers. They noted that while she was forced to convalesce over Christmas, she was remembered in the hospital by notables, including the Roosevelts. The diligent Caraway was probably comforted by the fact that being in the hospital over the Christmas holiday did not cause her to miss time in the Senate.

After a month-long convalescence, Caraway did eventually recover and was back at her Senate desk. It was a critical time in our nation's history as America drifted closer to the second global conflict of Caraway's lifetime.

To this day, many people remain under the mistaken impression that Hattie Caraway voted against America's entry into World War II. Nothing could be further from the truth. While she deplored war and the country's tendency to keep getting into it, she was a pragmatist and a patriot. All of her sons were West Pointers; two were on active duty and served with distinction during the war.

The vote for a declaration of war on December 8, 1941, passed 82 to 0 in the Senate, where Caraway served. In the House of Representatives, however, the vote was 388 to 1. The only dissenting House vote was cast by Representative Jeanette Rankin of Montana, who had also voted against the declaration of war in 1917 signaling America's entry into World War I. Because they were both women, one was confused with the other.

Yet even before America formally entered the war, Caraway had an interest in veterans and those in the military service. The *Batesville News Review* of June 24, 1941, stated, "Thousands of Veterans of Arkansas have been ably served by Mrs. Caraway at various times, and it is said that she has the most complete file on ex-service men of any United States senator in Washington."

The Batesville article went on to spotlight her support of the state's educational facilities and said, "When she becomes interested in any type of legislation, it is known that her influence is felt and carries much weight with her colleagues."

The same article went on to state, "She does not ask or give any odds because she is a woman. She is forceful, efficient and has served Arkansas well in the national Congress, and through her service, Arkansas has received national recognition."

Army Training, GI Bill

When America officially entered World War II, Caraway found a way to combine two causes she championed, education and military preparedness. The combination would benefit the good of the state's colleges as well as the war effort. She lobbied the federal government to establish military administration schools, college training detachments and other military training units on Arkansas' college campuses. Her actions were to have a ripple effect far into the future.

After the lean years of the Great Depression, enrollment at Arkansas colleges had already dropped precipitously due to lack of money for student tuition, scholarships and work-study stipends. The state of Arkansas provided little in the way of funding for its colleges and none at all for the construction of buildings. War would bring new setbacks.

Jonesboro's National Guard unit was activated in January 1941. Guardsmen who were students at Arkansas State had to withdraw from school. The official onset of the war in December 1941 saw most of the few remaining male students as well as faculty and staff members leave for the armed forces. Student deferments vanished. Female students left school for work in war industries or to marry their departing sweethearts. Old-timers recall that by 1943, there were only eleven male students left on the ASU campus. Since other local colleges had failed, and since there had already been a move in the Arkansas General Assembly to abolish state-supported colleges like that at Jonesboro, some worried that A-State might not be able to keep its doors open.

ASU historian Lee Dew stated, "The salvation of Arkansas State College during this period was the establishment of military training school on campus. The first of these schools was announced in December 1942 by President Kays. The first army facility on campus was a unit of the Army Administration School, the sixth such unit established in the nation, and the first in Arkansas. Much credit for securing the unit went to President Kays and Senator Hattie Caraway who contacted the War Department in June 1942 and offered the use of the facilities of the college."

By the following year, Caraway had succeeded in lobbying the War Department for A-State to also serve as one of the few locations in the nation for an Army College Training Detachment. Hundreds of soldiers from all over the country discovered Arkansas.

Rather than being applauded, Caraway observed in a letter at that time to V.C. Kays that success has many fathers: "I have just noted in the *Gazette*

Thanks to Hattie's efforts, soldiers from around the country, such as these from New York City, discovered Arkansas.

today that the Governor has taken full credit for the trainees in your school as well as all others in Arkansas."

With the full complement of GIs at Arkansas State, there were about two thousand soldiers training on campus. In the Army Air Corps flight training detachment, there were about three hundred cadets at any one time. For many, their time in Arkansas would be a brief respite to train before going on to D-Day, Iwo Jima, Okinawa. Many of them fell in love with Arkansas and its people, often marrying local girls and returning after the war to help build the state in the postwar prosperity.

A number of Arkansas schools benefited. As noted by Joe Lamb in Conway's *Log Cabin Democrat* on May 2, 2008, "During her time in the Senate, Caraway was instrumental in tripling the size of Arkansas State Teacher's College (now the University of Central Arkansas) from five major buildings to fifteen. Eight of the 10 new buildings still stand."

Army College Training Detachment at ASU in 1943.

Jimmy Bryant, UCA's director of Archives & Special Collections, concurred, stating that Caraway assisted the University of Central Arkansas in navigating through the system and receiving the proper financing. As with ASU, the state of Arkansas did not contribute any funds for construction at UCA. Also, as with ASU, buildings Caraway helped obtain for UCA are housing busy programs well into the twenty-first century.

Bryant said that UCA's president Heber McAlister worked closely with Caraway to receive funds to keep the college running. Because of this, Bryant said, "We were able to play a big role in World War II."

As at ASU, having military students on campus would not only aid in the war effort but also gain much-needed revenue for UCA. Naval cadets and air force cadets were housed on campus along with marine and naval reserves. A contingent of WAACs who called themselves Camp Conway became the largest of the groups at UCA, with 1,800 women being instructed during 1943–44 alone.

Then, as noted in the *Congressional Record* in 1944, Hattie Caraway joined Senator Champ Clark of Missouri in introducing a bill seeking federal financial aid for higher education and vocational training for returning veterans—the GI Bill of Rights. Of the thousands who came to Arkansas military training installations, many returned to the state after the war as college students under what came to be known popularly as the GI Bill.

FIGHTING FOR LIBERTY

In 1941, Arkansas would have lost one of its representatives in Congress had Caraway not stepped in to challenge the method of apportionment. She succeeded in looking out for her state. And she looked out for its most vulnerable, with old age pensions one of her continuing concerns. But she also had to look abroad.

The war years brought an entirely new set of challenges for Caraway. Whether due to the relatively straightforward nature of war compared to a complex economic disaster, or by her decade of experience in the Senate, through her sons or by her own native common sense, she was able to see the big picture.

In a 1941 radio address regarding the Lend-Lease bill for American aid to Britain, Caraway is nonplussed that people assumed she would think a certain way because of her gender:

> *I am the only woman member of the United States Senate. Because of that fact, I have received a great many communications against the bill that would not otherwise have come to me. They urge, that because of my sex, I should be in support of their views, vote against this proposed legislation....No bully is apt to attack one who is prepared...As a representative of a sovereign state, as an American mother, as one who has been a constant advocate of peace, as one who believes that humanity is at stake and that some measure must be taken to safeguard it, I cast my vote for the Lend-Lease bill.*

Even—or especially—in wartime, she remained a passionate champion of education. Her efforts were noted and appreciated. In 1942, the *State College Herald* said, "Senator Caraway has always been interested in the young people of America. She has made it possible for the youth of Arkansas to receive higher education and to reap benefits that they would not have received had it not been for her aid and support."

Most articles of the time spotlight both her contributions to education through the self-liquidating loans that made college building projects possible as well as her support of a strong military. They were combined in her efforts toward the ROTC unit at Arkansas State, which, its school newspaper said "came as a result of work in which our senior Senator had a large share."

The same newspaper applauded her efforts again two weeks later, on April 29, 1942, pointing out her support of FDR on measures that would put the country on a war production basis by voting for a large army, navy and air force.

Later that year, in November 1942, a Thanksgiving message by Caraway was significant enough to be carried in the *New York Times*. In it, she spoke to the women of occupied Europe in a message of hope during the "years of awful war." She cited her empathy with their plight, as her own two sons, both colonels in the army, were fighting for liberty in the midst of the conflict.

CROP OF GREATEST VALUE

While global hostilities were definitely on her mind, in 1943 Caraway was also looking ahead to the postwar world. She continued to press for federal aid to public education, stating that no bill that had come before the Senate during her term in office would affect the future of America more, having for its purpose "the proper educational training of our greatest national assets, the American youth of today and tomorrow."

She cited data showing America's painfully high illiteracy rate compared to both Germany and Japan, where illiteracy was almost nonexistent. She also referenced the number of men rejected for military service thus far in World War II due to lack of education, even during the time of America's greatest need. She compared the millions of dollars spent by the federal government on both war and agriculture, asking why at least an equal amount could not be spent on education for America's youth, "the crop of greatest value to our future."

Her years as both a schoolteacher and farm wife allowed her to clearly employ the metaphor. Communications expert Molly Mayhead concurs: "While she may not have spoken frequently, Caraway's carefully measured comments exuded commitment and an in-depth understanding of the issues."

Yet Caraway was not universally lauded by her contemporaries. Amy Porter in "Ladies of Congress," which was published in *Collier's* of August

28, 1943, notes in a not particularly favorable way that Caraway traveled to work by streetcar, often bringing her lunch. Porter calls her "conspicuously inconspicuous," adding that Caraway's favorite bill, "unsuccessfully introduced time and again," was a proposal requiring a parachute for every airline passenger. This contrasts with what Porter had to say about Representative Margaret Chase Smith, who is called hardworking, well-liked and a recipient of good committee assignments.

But Caraway was not out of the picture, nor were her issues trivial. As reflected in the *Congressional Record* in 1943, she made one of her rare speeches in the Senate. In it she was able to share the wisdom of someone who had been born in the decade after the Civil War and had seen World War I firsthand as a young mother. She asked her Senate colleagues to approve a proposal for a worldwide peacekeeping organization similar to the League of Nations, which had been rejected after World War I, and not to make the same mistakes yet again. In 1945, the Senate ratification of the United Nations Charter was delivered to the White House—by Garrett Whiteside.

EQUAL RIGHTS, SIMPLE PLEASURES

Caraway continued to be a supporter of FDR during the war years as she had been during the New Deal, endorsing Franklin Roosevelt's bids for a third and fourth term in 1940 and 1944, respectively.

By 1943, Hattie Caraway had been a United States senator for more than a decade. She was Arkansas' senior senator, serving with the same John McClellan whom she defeated for election in 1938. He had proclaimed then the need for another man in the Senate and even now referred to her achievement in presiding over the Senate as that of "a member of the gentle sex" rather than the senior senator from Arkansas.

Caraway at this time was still a most traditional woman. But in 1943, she co-sponsored an Equal Rights Amendment, a piece of legislation that had already been introduced in Congress eleven times. After some fine-tuning in committee, the proposal simply read, "Equality of rights under the law shall not be denied or abridged by the United States or by any State on account of sex."

She said her support was due to a desire to see women take more of a role in business, in the professions and in government, to assume greater responsibilities and "to work equally with men to build a better world." As in the past—and in the future—it did not pass.

Hattie (far right) with son Forrest; his wife, Betty (far left); and their daughter "Betsy," with unidentified woman, 1943. *Courtesy Caraway family.*

But the war years also held simple pleasures, including that of a first-time, doting grandmother. Caraway's granddaughter, Betty Caraway Hill, was born in 1940. Betty recalls that as a child, the family called her "Betsy," as reflected in Hattie's letters. Hattie often visited her hometown of Jonesboro and stayed with her friend Mrs. Parr, especially in the summer when Congress was in recess. There, she enjoyed small-town pleasures along with the kind of crises that were not touched upon in the Senate.

Mrs. Hill recalls, "We were in Jonesboro early in World War II. I was probably about three years old. I remember being at her house, apparently got bored and wandered out to a park down the block to watch a baseball game. The memory is somewhat vague, but I do recall hearing that everyone in town was looking for me."

Perhaps in order to keep her wandering granddaughter close to home, Hattie provided a special diversion. "I especially remember my grandmother's great big black purse," said Mrs. Hill. "It was about a foot long by eight inches and was a never-ending source of entertainment. I was allowed to go through it and remember finding treasures like her keys, wallet, etc."

Mrs. Hill remembers her grandmother's appearance and habits. "I never saw her in anything but black. But I do recall she had long red fingernails.

Hattie swinging granddaughter, Betsy, 1943. *Courtesy Caraway family.*

Doting grandmother Hattie holding Betsy, 1943. *Courtesy Caraway family.*

Backyard group, Hattie far right, 1943. *Courtesy Caraway family.*

She loved Garfinkle's white sale. She loved to go there, loved buying great big white linen napkins with her initials on them. Also, she always got caught in the rain without an umbrella, so she was always buying umbrellas."

Caraway always wore black, but she painted her long fingernails bright red. She was at all times a lady, but every now and then, a rebellious streak did manage to come out.

HATTIE SPEAKS

What did Hattie Caraway sound like at this time? In a rare recording made in her office during the 1940s, we are able to hear the cultured Southern voice of Senator Hattie Caraway during her final term. The recording was made by Bob Benson, who described himself as "curator of the National Voice Library."

In his introduction, Benson says Caraway was "a staunch FDR supporter who voted for much of the New Deal legislation." He also notes that she presided over a Senate session in substitution for the vice president and received a friendly note afterward from Roosevelt. Though the recording is undated, Caraway had presided over the Senate on October 19, 1943. The recording was most likely made between that date and December 19, 1944, her last day in the Senate. For the recording, this is what Caraway chose to say:

> *Because I am the first woman ever to have been elected to a full term in the United States Senate, I am asked to do a great many things of this kind. Upon the death of my husband in nineteen and thirty-one, the Governor of Arkansas appointed me for a sixty-day term. In a special election I was named to finish the unexpired term, then reelected for the full term of six years, defeating six men for the place. I serve on the following committees: Agriculture and Forestry, Commerce, the Library, and am chairman of the Committee on Enrolled Bills. I have enjoyed the work. The responsibility is very heavy. The nervous strain is great. But the contacts made and the feeling that by my role I can have a part in keeping our country the greatest democracy in the world is exceedingly interesting and worthwhile. I ask no special favors because I am a woman. The Senate, being what it is, grants no special favors. It is a good legislative arm of the government and all of us give of our best efforts to maintain it as such.*

Caraway was in demand and in press reports was called influential and respected. Occasionally, she had some female company in the Senate, but these were transitory and short-lived. Huey Long's widow, Rose McConnell Long of Louisiana, served for a year in 1936–37. Dixie Bibb Graves of Alabama served out an appointment for less than six months in 1937–38. Gladys Pyle of South Dakota served her appointment for less than two months in 1938–39.

But Hattie Caraway was a working senator who had remained consistently on the job since she was elected in her own right in 1932 and reelected in 1938. As the year 1944 approached, she had a decision to make.

Chapter 8

ALSO-RAN, GOING HOME

1944–1950

"Doing this on federal time so will stop."

O n February 1, 1943, her sixty-fifth birthday, Caraway announced her candidacy for reelection in the 1944 primary to be held on July 25. The other candidates were Governor Homer Adkins, El Dorado oilman T.H. Barton, Congressman J. William Fulbright, former congressman David Terry of Little Rock (who later withdrew) and, once again, J. Rosser Venable.

The next day, the *New York Times* reported that her only preparation for the campaign was buying a new hat. It showed. Her 1944 campaign has been described as "pitiful."

As in previous campaigns, she continued her refusal to attack opponents, instead concentrating on her record. She emphasized her work in flood control, federal aid to agriculture and education, securing old-age pensions and her efforts in the passage of the GI Bill of Rights.

Caraway signed the following "Dear Friend" campaign letter. Dated May 23, 1944, it lacks the forward-looking sense of the national mood that year. In fact, apart from references to the war, it is remarkably similar to her 1938 campaign piece. Perhaps her emphatic reference to supporting military preparedness is meant to help counter the continued false rumors that she voted against America's entry into World War II, when in fact it was the Republican Montana congresswoman, Jeanette Rankin. Note continued use of the "well known saying":

I shall greatly appreciate your help and influence in my race for reelection to the Senate. I am a ranking member of two powerful Committees which have much to do with the interests of Arkansas. They are Agriculture and Forestry, and Commerce. These Committee assignments are very valuable for the future of our State.

Since I have been in the Senate, my entire time and attention have been devoted to the duties of my office. It is said that mine is one of the best records of attendance both in the Senate and in the Committees where legislation is formed. I submit this record to the voters of my State. I feel that in the fight which I joined for preparedness, had enough of those in Congress joined with me and others in our effort our country would have been so prepared that Japan would not have dared to attack us. Some even go so far as to say that Hitler would not have gone to the lengths he did and brought on this awful war.

My two sons are in the service of their country, I know what this war means to them and to others in the service, as well as to their loved ones. I am doing what I can to aid them now and when the war is over, I will work for a lasting peace.

My office is subject "to call" to the people of Arkansas. It is a well known saying "Write Senator Caraway, she will help you if she can." Because of my length of service here which has given me experience and prominence in the Senate, I feel that I can serve the people better than one who does not possess these qualifications. In view of the fact that the Congress is remaining is session, I do not know how much time I can devote to campaigning without neglecting my duties here. It is my hope to go over the State and meet and greet as many as I can.

I am sure you know that I have done everything I possibly could to aid the schools of my State. I secured the first Federal loan for this purpose. The result was that of great benefit to the schools of my state and Nation. I am sure you also know I took the lead in the fight for Federal aid to education. If I am reelected, the teachers and schools in my State will have my continued support and friendship.

A somewhat more personal note to V.C. Kays followed the next month. Though sent in 1944, it was still lacking either excitement or the specifics he had advised her to use in the 1938 campaign: "I am writing asking for your support of my candidacy for reelection to the United States Senate. I am sure you know what a friend I have been to Arkansas State College and if I am reelected, I shall continue my efforts. For any assistance which you may render me, I shall be very grateful; and shall be pleased to hear from you at any time."

Ready for Change

Some say Caraway's candidacy was barely noticed. The real political fireworks in the 1944 campaign came from Fulbright and Adkins, which dated back to Fulbright's ouster as University of Arkansas president, as orchestrated by Adkins.

Another candidate, T.H. Barton, put on quite a show, literally. He was well financed and toured Arkansas with musical groups, including one from the Grand Ole Opry that included Minnie Pearl.

When the dust settled, Hattie Caraway came in fourth, with less than 14 percent of the vote. Only Venable came in behind her with 1 percent, in last place.

The thirty-nine-year-old Bill Fulbright (1905–1995) of Fayetteville won her Senate seat after a runoff against her former ally and later opponent, Adkins. It was on the political battle between those two men that the race had centered. Hattie was simply an "also-ran."

Upon her crushing defeat, Caraway's only known public response was simply, "The people are speaking." Yet her letters reveal she was hurt and bitter. Perhaps she was able to take some small comfort in the fact that one year later, Britain's wartime hero Winston Churchill was also defeated in his bid for reelection. Political analysts have stated that people were just ready for a change.

However, without Long or Adkins as advisors, Caraway's campaign strategy may have been too generalized. In 1938, Kays had warned her to be specific about her achievements. Many women, perhaps especially those raised to be ladies of the South, are reluctant to sing their own praises. What may be seen as proof of accomplishment in a man might be interpreted by some as boastful in a woman.

Perhaps Caraway personified the kind of modesty of her era espoused by her contemporary, MGM movie producer Irving Thalberg. He did not allow his name to be listed on his films as others did, saying, "Credit you give yourself isn't worth having."

Yet apart from her one-on-one efforts for individuals, there were indeed major accomplishments for Caraway during the war years as there were during the Depression. Her wartime achievements went beyond the military training schools at Arkansas colleges. These included being instrumental in securing Camp Robinson in North Little Rock as an army training center, Fort Smith's Camp Chaffee, ordnance plants and aluminum factories in Arkansas during World War II.

Perhaps people forgot Caraway's role in those projects or simply never knew. Or perhaps people really were just ready for a change.

The U.S. Senate website quotes journalist Drew Pearson commenting on the final stages of her Senate career: "In that turbulent chamber, where a person's good points or bad quickly shine through the gloss, [Hattie Caraway] held her own."

On December 19, 1944, which was to be her last day in office, Democratic senator Carl Hatch of New Mexico made a glowing speech about her, asking fellow senators to honor her with a rare standing ovation. The *Congressional Record* notes Hatch as saying, "The Senator from Arkansas is not present, but I hope the *Record* will show that every Senator present rose and applauded."

Why was Caraway absent? For someone with an outstanding record of attendance in the Senate, it was a highly unusual aberration, especially on that day of all days. Did she fear the moment might cause her eyes to well with tears, thus branding her the kind of "emotional woman" that she had worked so hard to avoid? Even in our enlightened times, women are extremely wary of shedding tears at the workplace. Caraway, always in the spotlight and always mindful of displaying "too much or too little," could hardly have been less so.

CONTINUED TO SERVE

Did Hattie ever talk about what it was like for her to be in the Senate? "There were times when she really did enjoy it," said granddaughter Mrs. Hill.

Though Caraway was defeated in the 1944 election, she remained in public service, shuttling between Washington and New York City. She was appointed by President Franklin Roosevelt to the Federal Employees' Compensation Commission, serving until 1946, when President Harry Truman appointed her to the Employees' Compensation Appeals Board.

Upon Hattie Caraway's departure from the Senate in 1945, Garrett Whiteside was appointed the Senate's Clerk of Enrolled Bills. But according to the *New York Times*, within two years, "he was retired as the result of the reorganization by the Republicans." He survived the loss of his job for only four months.

After his forced retirement on March 1, 1947, Whiteside wrote a current events column for the *Arkansas Democrat*. But on July 2, 1947, Whiteside was listening to a baseball game on the radio at his home in Washington when he suffered a heart attack and died before a doctor could arrive. He was sixty-two years old.

Whiteside's passing was considered noteworthy enough to be cited prominently in a lengthy obituary with a photo in the *New York Times*. It carried the subhead, "Secretary Handled Detailed Work on Last 2 War Declarations—Called '97th Senator.'"

By 1946, World War II was fully over and people tried to put it behind them even as Winston Churchill's "Iron Curtain" speech warned of things to come. Caraway was working at her new job, which took her to New York, a place she did not enjoy.

The sole Christmas greeting Caraway received in 1946 from her former Congressional colleagues was from Representative William Fadjo Cravens of Fort Smith, in Garrett Whiteside's home district.

Even after she left office, however, Hattie Caraway was known. "Once she took me to meet Harry Truman, and I got to sit on his lap," said Betty Caraway Hill. "She had no problem getting in to see important people."

And while there were few red carpets back then, Mrs. Hill said, "I remember once in Kansas City when we were living at Fort Leavenworth, Kansas. She took me to the premiere of the film *The Red Shoes* [1948]. The press people were there at the premiere looking for celebrities, and I guess she was the only one, so they asked her why she came. She said, 'I came to take my granddaughter to the movies.'"

In this letter to V.C. Kays on January 3, 1946, she referred to her son Forrest; his wife, Betty; and to Betsy, a nickname for their daughter, Mrs. Hill. Even at age sixty-eight, Caraway was thinking about weight.

> *Just a word of greeting in this new year of 1946. It seems so long since I have heard from you. It was a very welcome sight to see your Christmas wishes. I'm such a poor correspondent. I went to Washington on Friday before Christmas and returned here on New Year's Day.*
>
> *Forrest is back from the war looking very fit, and without a scratch. He and Betty came to Washington about 2 weeks before Christmas and are in my apartment. So far, they have not found a place to live. Betsy is five and a half now and weighs 65 pounds. She does not eat terribly much...It seems to me I remember I was something of a fat little girl when I was her age.*

I don't know whether our representatives went home for Christmas or not. I had a card from Fadjo and his wife, but just silence from the others.

I'm awfully glad the war is over. We never learn, even from experience. I have a good job here, and enjoy the work, but New York is too big for me. I never will like it. Must stop—sometime when you have time, drop me a line. I'd love to hear from you all. Good wishes for your new year.

GOING HOME

In a letter to Kays from Caraway on January 3, 1947, it is touching to read of her being too late to place her Christmas order at Sears. At that time, she had access to the nation's most iconic department stores in New York City. Remarkably, three years after the fact, Caraway's 1944 election defeat was still in her thoughts as seen in her apparent non sequitur. "Bill" is J. William Fulbright, who then held her Senate seat. She was still conscientious about her work.

I had your card and was delighted to hear from you. I failed to put in my order from Sears this year until too late. I was busy and upset in my mind. So I let the time pass. I am doing very well in my job if I am allowed to keep it—not being a policy-making body makes me hopeful.

What did you think of Bill wanting us to go to the British form of government? I think Truman should have called him in and told him to go over to the Republican party or keep his mouth shut.

Of course, I was hurt by not getting more votes than I did, but am glad I am out of the mess [emphasis the author's].

Doing this on federal time so will stop. When you have the time, drop me a line—I'd love to see you both. Happy new year.

In three years, she would be dead. Caraway suffered a stroke in January of 1950 that left her partially paralyzed. According to the Associated Press, she was a patient at Walter Reed Army Hospital before being moved to White Hall Sanitarium at nearby Falls Church, Virginia, where her condition declined. According to the AP, she died at age seventy-two on December 21, 1950, at 11:05 a.m.

She was buried in Jonesboro five days later. President Harry Truman sent condolences. An obituary appeared on page 23 of the *New York Times*

Caraway family gravesite in Jonesboro.

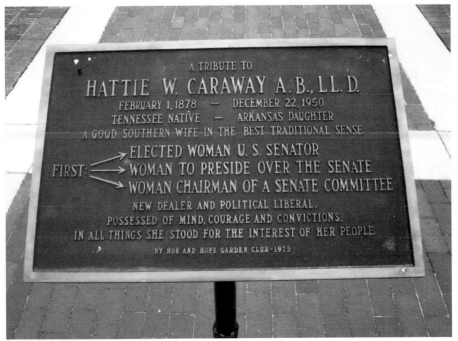

Plaque honoring Hattie Caraway at the Craighead County Courthouse in Jonesboro.

with a headline that almost overwhelmed the obituary itself: "HATTIE CARAWAY, EX-SENATOR, DIES; First Woman Ever Elected to Post, She Succeeded Her Husband Late in 1931, Served Two Full Terms, Won National Reputation, Presided Over Senate Session."

Hattie Caraway grave marker in Jonesboro.

Caraway's passing was also recognized by the Associated Press wire through which it was carried by various newspapers across the country. There were also some local obituaries in Arkansas. Yet for the most part, her passing went generally unnoticed.

But for more than a dozen years, she had been one of the most famous women in America. Today, many people owe a debt of gratitude to this mostly unsung woman from history, whether they realize it or not. Upon becoming the first woman to be elected as a United States senator, Hattie Wyatt Caraway, at age fifty-four, forced herself to quickly learn what she needed to do to help people during the Great Depression and World War II. Then, she used what tools she had to their best advantage.

Today she lies with her husband, Thad, and their son Robert in a simple gravesite at Jonesboro's Oaklawn Cemetery. She is back home among the people she never forgot.

POSTSCRIPT

Caraway always remained a friend to her home state, and her legacy lives on, whether people know it or not. Four of the nine buildings she helped obtain for Arkansas State University during the depths of the Depression are still heavily used today, including the current College of Business, College of Nursing and Health Professions, the Art Annex and Department of Math and Computer Science. Seven of the ten she helped bring about at the University of Central Arkansas are still being used: Bernard Hall, McAlister Hall, McCastlain Hall, Ida Waldran Auditorium, Wingo Hall, the President's Home and Prince Center.

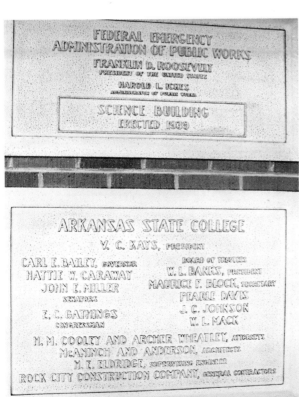

Above: ASU Business Building, one of nine obtained with Caraway's help, still heavily used today.

Left: Science Building plaque, at the current ASU College of Business.

Both schools educate tens of thousands of students each year. Would the schools have continued to grow without Caraway and the facilities and military training programs she helped make possible?

Hundreds of teachers graduate from both schools year after year, going on to educate the children of the state and the nation. What a fitting tribute to Caraway, the former schoolteacher who knew the transformative power of education as the road out of poverty.

Generation after generation, Caraway's legacy lives on.

In 1993, Arkansas senators Dale Bumpers and David Pryor proposed that a portrait of Hattie Caraway be commissioned for the Senate wing of the U.S. Capitol. Arkansas painter John Oliver Buckley was selected for the commission. The oil on canvas portrait of Caraway was unveiled at the U.S. Capitol in 1996. With the kind permission of the Senate curator, it graces the cover of this book.

Until a portrait of Senator Margaret Chase Smith was commissioned in 1999, the only two women to have been so honored were Pocahontas and Hattie Caraway.

In 2001, Hattie Caraway was featured on a postage stamp. She was only the third person to be featured in the Postal Service's Distinguished Americans series, following General Joseph Stillwell and Senator Claude Pepper. Caraway's stamp was seventy-six cents, drawn by Canadian artist Mark Summers. One collector stated that the Caraway stamp was probably the first U.S. postage stamp depicting an Arkansas resident for what he or she accomplished in Arkansas.

It was unveiled at the State Capitol in Little Rock on February 21 and again the following day in her hometown of Jonesboro. Senator Blanche Lincoln spoke at both events, having followed in Caraway's footsteps by being the second woman elected to the U.S. Senate from Arkansas.

In the book *Nine and Counting*, Lincoln cites Caraway as a role model for her own Senate career. Lincoln was well aware of Hattie Caraway's place in history as well as her own by following in those footsteps. During Lincoln's Senate campaign, a Caraway Club for female supporters was formed, emulating those of the same name during Hattie's 1932 run for office.

After the 2012 election, a total of twenty women would be serving in the United States Senate, the most ever. An unexpected challenge arose. As previously noted, a restroom for female senators was not provided until 1993. It contained two cubicles. News media in November 2012 breathlessly reported that now, for the first time, there was a traffic jam at the Senate women's bathroom. It was far too small.

This news might have brought a silent, enigmatic smile from the woman who started it all: Arkansas senator Hattie Caraway.

STUDENT COMMONS
BUILDING
ERECTED A·D·1936
FEDERAL EMERGENCY ADMINISTRATION
OF PUBLIC WORKS
PROJECT NO · 3726

FRANKLIN D · ROOSEVELT
PRESIDENT OF THE UNITED STATES

HATTIE W · CARAWAY
JOSEPH T · ROBINSON
SENATORS

WILLIAM J · DRIVER
CONGRESSMAN

A · N · McANINCH
ARCHITECT

NEWTON H · BROWN
CONSULTING ENGINEER

H · E · ELDRIDGE
SUPERVISING ENGINEER

O · H · BURDEN COMPANY
GENERAL CONTRACTORS

Above: ASU Nursing Building, brought about by Caraway, still heavily used today.

Left: Plaque for the Commons Building, now the ASU College of Nursing and Health Professions.

107

Above: ASU Mathematics & Computer Science Building, formerly Teacher Training facility, made possible by former schoolteacher Hattie Caraway.

Left: Teacher Training Building plaque, at the current ASU Department of Math and Computer Science.

Chapter 9

FROM THE LAST ROW

"I feel so alone—so bad indeed—but I shall hold on to my courage."

Perhaps it was holding Hattie Caraway's actual writings. The sturdy penmanship seemed to underscore the earnestness she put into her work. Perhaps it was also reading now-yellowed newspapers from her day, seeing how esteemed she was held by her contemporaries. She came alive and deserved someone to speak for her instead of simply being dismissed as "silent."

There is no question that the mass of early journal entries primarily dallied on clothes, food, frugality and overeating. "Went to Luncheon. Furnished coffee. Had Tongue—Ham—dill pickles—avocado salad—grapefruit—and waldorf salad—sunshine, angel and chocolate cake—I overate." Or this entry that any parent can recognize as her son came for lunch: "That kid ordered a $1.15 steak. The lunch cost me $3.95 & .40 tips making $4.35. I can't stand that often."

As many women have found through the ages, a journal was a way of expressing thoughts that could not be verbalized among men. Having no real confidants, it was one of Hattie's few outlets.

It is also probable that Caraway had reason to believe the journal of the first woman elected to the Senate might be good copy for publication at a later time. Most likely, she probably felt it would be suitable for one of the women's magazines of the day.

Perusing a random selection of such magazines from the 1930s as well as those of today reveals a shocking truth. While the women's magazines of Hattie's day concentrated for the most part on clothes and food, most of today's women's magazines concentrate on…clothes and food. She was writing for the marketplace.

Some readers may snicker at her provincialisms, such as: "Hooee!! Somebody's shirt is torn." Certainly, there are enough such moments in the journal to guarantee mirth at her expense. However, she clearly notes that she meant to edit it if it was ever published. Who would want their private diary exposed for the world to see without the chance to revise it?

Today, her stand against anti-lynching, anti–poll tax and repeal of Prohibition are indefensible. In the former two cases, she stood with almost every other Southern senator and maintained it was a "states' rights" issue. Equally likely was her statement that she tried to vote as "Dad" would have done, her late husband, Thad, whose racial views were well known. Regarding Prohibition, it is interesting to note that at this writing, her hometown of Jonesboro and Craighead County, Arkansas, are still dry.

Some deride her repeated—and quite unsuccessful—proposal requiring a parachute for every airplane passenger. Yet it may not have been as ludicrous as it sounds today. The slower propeller-driven planes of that era occasionally did run out of fuel or suffer mechanical failure while airborne. The Caterpillar Club, named for the silk from which the chutes were made, was formed in 1922. Complete with pin and certificate, its members were fliers whose lives were saved by using a parachute when forced to jump from their planes. By the mid-1940s, the Caterpillar Club had more than thirty-four thousand members. At the very least, the presence of parachutes might have comforted people when passenger air travel was in its infancy. Many legislators have a questionable "pet" issue; Hattie's was for the good of others, not self-enrichment or a trip to the pork barrel.

No Predecessors, No Mentors

Hattie Caraway was a trailblazer just by being in the Senate for more than one day. She had no predecessors from whom to learn, no mentors to guide her. Joe T. Robinson, her Arkansas colleague, was little help. She liked and respected Robinson, since Thad had done so. The same for Huey Long. Perhaps what Hattie wanted from Robinson was simply a small measure of respect. She had to know she was not a nationally prestigious figure like him, but for better or worse, she was still a duly elected fellow senator, and she tried hard to do her best as well as not to be an embarrassment.

She was named a delegate to the Democratic National Convention in both 1936 and 1944. At convention of 1936, Hattie Caraway was chosen to make the seconding speech for Franklin Delano Roosevelt's presidential nomination. Would they have trusted the national stage to someone who was an embarrassment, especially for a luminary like FDR, even to woo the so-called "female vote"?

Certainly Hattie Caraway was lacking in many attributes of those women who followed her into the Senate, such as the stateliness of Margaret Chase Smith or the star power of Hillary Rodham Clinton. But the key word is "followed." Hattie had no one before her, no mentors and few friends. Yet she succeeded.

In her journal of May 12, 1932, just after she had declared her intention to run for the full term, she showed her determination: "I really have very great admiration for the time and real effort expended by these men. I'm working as hard, and trying to understand. If the people of my state continue me here, I shall not regret the long hours, nor the mental strain…My, I feel so alone—so bad indeed—but I shall hold on to my courage."

Like any man, Hattie Caraway used the tools available to her; they were just different tools. She knew she was not a sophisticate. For her, a watershed event was buying a black petticoat in Washington. Prior to that, she had been affectionately mocked in her hometown of Jonesboro for often appearing downtown with her white slip showing beneath her black dress. Even today, some of Jonesboro's senior citizens recall their mothers admonishing them, "Well, Miss Hattie!" if their slips drooped below their hemlines.

But Caraway was also a lone woman caught between two of the most powerful men of her time, Joe T. Robinson and Huey Long. She emerged unscathed, without alienating either of them. And she survived them both.

BLACK DRESS, RED NAILS

Hattie Caraway was born in the rural South in the shadow of the Civil War. She had been a farm wife. She was fifty-four years old when she entered the Senate. Unlike today, when fifty-four might be considered "the new forty," she showed her years. She did not photograph well. She was tiny, round, loved to eat and was hardly stylish. Some called her dour and dowdy. But while she famously always wore black, she painted her long fingernails bright red.

She recognized when she was marginalized and when a snub was a snub. She knew women were expected to remain in their place, and for the most part, she quietly did so. She then had to accept being derided as "Silent Hattie" for doing just that.

But she also recognized that a person of moderate intelligence who worked hard and who stayed awake at their Senate desk might be just as useful to the country as those who made bombastic speeches. She was criticized for knitting, reading Zane Gray novels or the newspaper and working crossword puzzles during the incessant Senate speeches. But she saw the men visiting with each other, asleep at their desks or not even showing up.

She rarely missed a vote or a committee meeting, did not take time away from the Senate to campaign and started each day reading every word of the *Congressional Record*. Did Hattie threaten to expose the Great Secret of the Senate, the self-styled "world's most exclusive club"? Could a reasonably intelligent person without wealth, connections or an elite education do the job and do it without self-interest? What would happen to our legislative system if one of the two senators from each state were an average person with an average income, who knew the price of milk and bread and who remembered there were people who had less?

MYTHS

There have been a number of myths repeated about Hattie Caraway. The first, of course, was that she was ineffectual. Perhaps some of the material in this volume has at least offered a glimpse into an alternate view.

Some denounce her for voting against America's entry into World War II. It was, in fact, another woman of another party in another legislative body, as is clearly shown in Senate records.

Some claim that Caraway broke her promise not to run for a full term. Nowhere has it been substantiated that she promised anyone at any time. She pointedly denied it. Much, however, has been written of the men simply being "confident" that she would not run.

Other myths were apparently invented and then reprinted in the press. One was that Caraway's first words upon entering the Senate Chamber were, "The windows need washing." According to Betty Koed, Senate historian, "There were no windows in the Senate Chamber in 1932. In fact, the current chamber (occupied since 1859) has never had windows. It is a completely interior room. Of course, all the surrounding spaces, such as the Senate Reception Room, the hallway outside the chamber, and so forth have large windows. She could very well have been referring to those windows. She also had an office in the Russell Senate Office Building, which has large windows."

But the Senate Chamber was specified. It does at least stretch the imagination to believe that someone like Caraway—who took her position so seriously and who knew that, as the only woman, she'd be quoted—would allow the first words out of her mouth as a senator to be critical, clichéd and petty-minded.

A widespread reproach of Caraway during the 1932 campaign was that she was needed at home to take care of her children. Since her sons were West Pointers and army officers, it is hard to know how much of a mother's care they required.

It is interesting to speculate what her response might have been to the catastrophic fire that burned Arkansas State University's Main Building to the ground in 1931. When contacted by college president V.C. Kays, Thad Caraway's response was short, mildly sympathetic and absolutely no help. What might Hattie have done? Her assistance to Arkansas' colleges while in office to obtain federal construction funds at least poses the possibility that she might have tried to do more at that critical time.

Today, thousands of students benefit from the buildings that resulted from her work. But who remembers the speeches that were being made in the Senate by others while she was doing it?

She was roundly panned for not making speeches in the Senate. Yet, if you were a veteran needing benefits, an elderly person needing your pension or a young person needing an education, what might have been more helpful? Would you rather have your problem solved or have someone make a speech about it?

Hattie Caraway had no guidance in her new role, but she succeeded. Certainly many say with some justification that she would not have won in 1932 without Huey Long or in 1938 without Homer Adkins. Yet, ultimately it was the voters of Arkansas who decided. There are also those who say, again not unrealistically, that the six-man race in 1932 split the vote, but Caraway also won in 1938 against the formidable John McClellan.

She was not perfect. She was not exemplary in every way. She was not a role model in today's usage. But she was also not ineffectual, she was not incompetent and she was not an embarrassment. In her own words, "My idea of the job is to do my level best to represent the people of my state not

only in matters of legislation but in all matters where I can be of service."
At that, she succeeded.

TRUE LEGACY

One day in 2002, over a half century after Caraway's death, the author was sitting next to Arkansas senator Blanche Lincoln at a speaking engagement. The senator chanced to open her daily planner. Inside the front cover where she would see it each day, Senator Lincoln had boldly written, "If I can hold on to my sense of humor and a modicum of dignity I shall have had a wonderful time running for office, whether I get there or not"—Hattie W. Caraway.

As the author was in costume for a presentation as Hattie Caraway, it was a golden moment.

Caraway had many achievements that refute being called ineffectual. Though mocked for her parachute proposal, Caraway also co-sponsored the GI Bill and an Equal Rights Amendment. She found construction funding for buildings that doubled or tripled the size of Arkansas college campuses, enabling thousands of teachers and nurses, among others, to serve their state. She increased the number of roads and bridges and hospitals in a state that didn't have many. She directly helped innumerable individuals whose old age pensions, veterans' benefits, work relief and education were hopelessly stalled.

Most of all, Hattie Caraway, in her unpretentious way, showed that regardless of gender, age, background, training, career, education or other qualifier, a person can enter public service and be useful to his or her community, state and country.

Perhaps that, then, is the true legacy of Hattie Caraway.

How "Silent" Was Hattie?

An oft-noted quote from Hattie Caraway seems to resonate strongly with many women to this day. After an exchange with Arkansas' senior senator, Joe T. Robinson, she confided to her journal, "Guess I said too much or too little. Never know."

As Arkansas State Representative Donna Hutchinson said in her paper, *The Not So Silent Hattie Caraway*, "These simple words in Hattie Caraway's journal express the thoughts of many women entering the field of politics."

In the Senate, Caraway remained cordial with her colleagues and did not "rock the boat." Hutchinson points out that the Senate in those days did not have a microphone. To make a speech, a woman would have to shriek to be heard. Caraway was smart enough to know that was not the way to do it.

She listened attentively to other senators' speeches, worked quietly, considered the issues and voted with colleagues when she could. However, even Huey Long, to whom she owed so much, found he could not count on her being a rubber stamp for his agenda. She voted independently, according to her conscience and her constituents.

She did some of her best work in Senate committees where she could speak in normal tones, proving herself to be pleasant, prepared and politically savvy. She not only gained the respect of her colleagues in this smaller forum but also managed to get things done. She knew about issues like flood control and agricultural problems because she'd seen them with her own eyes.

It is in observing her colleagues on the floor of the Senate that the germ of an idea may have formed. While her reasons for making the shocking decision to run for a full term of her own in 1932 may be complex, at least part of it had to be because she saw her male colleagues acting uncouth, dressing sloppily, speaking poorly, lapsing in attendance and sleeping at their desks. Perhaps her "theory" was that a woman with common sense could be just as good as a man in the Senate—and certainly no worse.

In dealing with her male colleagues, what she did apparently worked. On her last day in the Senate, they gave her a remarkable standing ovation. She also received from a colleague what was no doubt intended as a compliment: "Mrs. Caraway is the kind of woman Senator that men Senators prefer."

As a woman in the Senate, she was the only one of her kind. In most ways, she was very much of her time and of the South. She was raised not only to be a lady but also a Southern lady. While for the most part she was ignored in the Senate, one false move would be noticed by all. She had to avoid any missteps or being seen as a threat, an alien presence disturbing the peace in what has been called the Ultimate Boys' Club.

Communications expert Dr. Kathleen Hall Jamieson refers to the double-bind problems that females face in politics as well as in the board room. Jamieson says female leaders cannot afford to appear weak, emotional or indecisive. But neither can they be seen as shrill or aggressive, which usually leads to being marginalized or maligned in unflattering, sometimes vulgar, terms.

If she's too quiet, she will be ignored. If she's too bold, she may be a threat and therefore undermined. Caraway chose discretion. She then had to bear the pejorative nickname "Silent Hattie" and face criticism by political opponents for not making enough speeches. But she got the job done.

Perhaps she thought making fifteen speeches in the Senate was enough, especially if she saved them for important issues. Perhaps she consciously determined how best to handle a unique situation. Perhaps she simply used the tools available to her in uncharted waters to navigate between being ineffective on one hand and alienating her colleagues on the other.

Or perhaps she simply asked herself if desperate people would benefit more from her help in getting food, jobs, healthcare and education or by making speeches about their troubles. Perhaps by keeping "silent," she allowed her voice—and more importantly, theirs—to be heard.

Appendix II

REELECT SENATOR HATTIE CARAWAY

This 1938 Caraway campaign piece should be a fairly accurate representation of Hattie Caraway's efforts as a senator; it would have been publicly challenged by her opponent if it was not. Far from being ineffective, the specifics would seem to confirm her diligence. The sentence near the bottom speaks volumes: "It is a well known saying in Arkansas: 'Write Senator Caraway. She will help you, if she can.'"

One of the most important offices to be filled in the primary election is that of United States senator, for which Hattie W. Caraway is a candidate for a second term.

When Senator Caraway made the race for election, she stated that she was for legislation for the relief of those who really needed relief; the ones who were losing their homes; those who had lost their jobs and farmers who could not get the cost of production for their products. She promised to do what she could to help the workers, and to work for the betterment of her state and the nation.

Senator Caraway has kept the faith and made good her promises. She has become known as one of the champions of the common people, as was her illustrious husband, the late Thaddeus H. Caraway.

AGRICULTURE AND FORESTRY. Senator Caraway was reared on a farm and knows the problems of the farmer. Arkansas being largely an agricultural state, and knowing the value of that committee to Arkansas, she asked and received an assignment to the Committee on Agriculture and Forestry. As a member of that committee, she has helped prepare many measures for the benefit of the farmer.

FLOOD CONTROL. Arkansas having more miles of navigable streams than any other state, she secured an appointment to the Committee on Commerce, which handles flood control legislation in that body. As a member of that committee, she has assisted in preparing important legislation on this subject, and has secured millions of dollars in appropriations for that work in Arkansas.

OTHER COMMITTEES. Senator Caraway is also a member of the Committee on the Library and Enrolled Bills. As Chairman of the last named committee, she has handled thousands of legislative measures without an error.

COMMITTEE WORK. An experienced observer who attends meetings of the committees has said that Senator Caraway knew better what she desired for her constituents than any other member of the committees upon which she served.

RECORD OF ATTENDANCE. The records of the committees and the Senate show that Senator Caraway has one of the best records of attendance upon their meetings.

LABOR. Senator Caraway is regarded as one of the staunchest friends of Labor in the Senate. She has been endorsed by numerous labor organizations.

EDUCATION. Senator Caraway is known as a friend to education and has consistently supported legislation for the improvement of education of the boys and girls of Arkansas and the nation. She secured the first federal loan for Arkansas made to any state in the Union, and thousands of our men and women have benefited by this act. She has also secured many Works Progress Administration projects for schools. She has aided in securing large grants of federal money to carry on the schools of Arkansas. Her work along this line has been of untold benefit to students in her state, as well as to the school teachers.

NATIONAL YOUTH ADMINISTRATION. Senator Caraway was one of the original supporters of the work of the National Youth Administration, which has aided so many girls and boys to better prepare themselves for life.

CIVILIAN CONSERVATION CORPS. Senator Caraway was one of the first who favored and worked for the Civilian Conservation Corps, which has aided thousands of young men and women and veterans and their families. She has secured many of these camps for Arkansas.

PUBLIC WORKS ADMINISTRATION. There are few, if any, projects of this administration, which Senator Caraway has not secured or helped to secure for her state. This includes many improvements such as public buildings, hospitals, water systems, etc. She was one of the leaders in securing the loan for the State Hospital at Benton.

EMPLOYMENT. Through her support of the Works Progress Administration and similar agencies, she has not only aided in securing employment for thousands of Arkansans, but it has resulted in hundreds of projects of permanent value to our state. More than once she has been largely responsible in keeping needy men and women employed in this work.

VETERANS. Senator Caraway is regarded as one of the best friends of veterans and their families in the Senate. She has worked and voted for many laws for the betterment of ex-servicemen and their dependents. She was a leader in the fight for the Bonus. Her office has over twenty thousand claims of individual veterans, the largest in Congressional offices.

SERVICE TO STATE. There is not a member of the Senate more ready to help her constituents than is Senator Caraway. No service is too small, and none too large, but that she will not give her best efforts to aid. She receives as much, if not more correspondence, than any member of the Senate. It is a well known saying in Arkansas: "Write Senator Caraway. She will help you, if she can."

The eyes of the nation and the world are upon the state of Arkansas in this race, for Sen. Caraway is one of the most famous women in the world. She is experienced and qualified...The people of Arkansas can perform no greater service to their state than by re-electing Senator Hattie W. Caraway to a second term in the United States Senate.

Senate Tribute to
Hattie Caraway

MR. HATCH: Mr. President, while sitting here this afternoon and listening to several farewell speeches, the idea occurred to me that we were about to lose many close associations and friendships. I shall not attempt to enumerate them all. I see present the Senator from Missouri [MR. CLARK]. Just a moment ago I saw the Senator from Oregon [MR. HOLMAN], and other Senators who are about to depart and will not be with us at the beginning of the next Congress. Of course, to all those Senators I express, not only for myself, but I am sure for the vast majority of Senators, our regrets that they will not be with us again.

But it occurred to me that possibly Senators had overlooked the fact that there is leaving us this afternoon, not to return again, the only lady Senator, MRS. HATTIE W. CARAWAY, the Senator from Arkansas. To her I wish to pay a brief tribute.

Mrs. Caraway has been a Member of the Senate longer than I have. She has always been most gracious, most kindly, and most ladylike. If I may be forgiven for saying so, inasmuch as I believe that her votes throughout the years since I have been here have corresponded almost exactly with mine, I am tempted to say that the Senator from Arkansas has been most statesmanlike in the votes she has cast.

So, without regard to the gentlemen who are leaving the Senate and will not return, I think it would be a very fitting thing for us, who are men, to stand for a moment and give a handclap for the Senator from Arkansas [MRS. CARAWAY]. May it be done?

[The senators rose in their places and applauded.]

MR. HATCH: Mr. President, the Senator from Arkansas is not present, but I hope the *Record* will show that every Senator present rose and applauded.

Sources

Buckingham, David E. "Shaggy Coats and True Friends." *The Rotarian*, November 1935.

Caraway, Hattie. Hattie Wyatt Caraway Papers. Special Collections, University of Arkansas–Fayetteville.

———. *Journal*. In Hattie Wyatt Caraway Papers. Special Collections, University of Arkansas–Fayetteville.

"Caraway Will Address Seniors." *Arkansas State College Herald*, April 29, 1942.

Congressional Record. 78th Congress, 3rd session, 1944, 90, pt. 7:9775.

"Congresswoman Is Well Pleased With Sorority." *Arkansas State College Herald*, March 9, 1938.

Crawford, Julienne. "Hattie Ophelia Wyatt Caraway (1878–1950)." *Encyclopedia of Arkansas.* www.encyclopediaofarkansas.net/encyclopedia/entry (accessed December 6, 2012).

Creel, George. "The Woman Who Holds Her Tongue." *Collier's*, September 18, 1937.

Davis, Maxine. "Five Democratic Women." *Ladies' Home Journal*, May 1933.

Deutsch, Hermann B. "Hattie and Huey." *Saturday Evening Post*, October 15, 1932.

———. *The Huey Long Murder Case.* Garden City, NY: Doubleday, 1963.

Dew, Lee A. *The ASU Story: A History of Arkansas State University 1909–1967.* Jonesboro: Arkansas State University Press, 1968.

Dunn, Susan. *Roosevelt's Purge: How FDR Fought to Change the Democratic Party.* Cambridge, MA: Belknap Press of Harvard University Press, 2010.

Hair, William Ivy. *The Kingfish and His Realm: The Life and Times of Huey P. Long.* Baton Rouge: Louisiana State University Press, 1996.

"Hattie W. Caraway." In *Current Biography 1945.* New York: H.W. Wilson and Co., 1945.

"Hattie Wyatt Caraway: A Woman of Conviction." *National Business Woman*, January 1979.

Henderson, Amber. "New Stamp Features Arkansas' Hattie Caraway." *Jonesboro Sun*, January 5, 2001.

Hutchinson, Donna. "The Not So Silent Hattie Caraway." Paper presented at the panel *From Spouses to Candidates: Radicalizing the Roots of the Political System through the Management of Rhetorical Roles.* National Communication Association. Atlanta, Georgia, November 21–24, 2001.

James, Edward T. *Notable American Women, 1607–1950.* Cambridge, MA: Harvard University Press, 1971.

Kays Collection. Archives and Special Collections, Arkansas State University–Jonesboro.

Kelly, Patrick. "Hattie Caraway." *Arkansas Democrat,* July 22, 1984.

Kincaid, Diane. *Silent Hattie Speaks: The Personal Journal of Senator Hattie Caraway.* Westport, CT: Greenwood Press, 1979.

Knable, Kate. "'Silent Hattie' Quiet But Effective." *Arkansas Business,* March 29, 2010.

Lamb, Joe. "Arkansas Political History on Display." *Log Cabin Democrat,* May 2, 2008.

Ledbetter, Calvin R. "The Other Caraway: Senator Thaddeus H. Caraway." *Arkansas Historical Quarterly* LXIV, no. 2 (Summer 2005).

Long, Huey P. *Every Man a King: The Autobiography of Huey P. Long.* Cambridge, MA: Da Capo Press, 1996.

Malone, David. *Hattie and Huey: An Arkansas Tour.* Fayetteville: University of Arkansas Press, 1989.

Mayhead, Molly, and Brenda DeVore Marshall. *Women's Political Discourse: A 21st Century Perspective.* Lanham, MD: Rowman & Littlefield Publishers, 2005.

Paxton, Annabel. *Women in Congress.* Richmond, VA: Dietz Press, 1945.

Porter, Amy. "Ladies of Congress." *Collier's,* August 28, 1943.

Stevens, Peter E. *The Mayflower Murderer and Other Forgotten Firsts in American History.* New York: William Morrow, 1993.

Towns, Stuart. "A Louisiana Medicine Show: The Kingfish Elects an Arkansas Senator." *Arkansas Historical Quarterly* XXV, 1966.

Weller, Cecil Edward. *Joe T. Robinson: Always a Loyal Democrat.* Fayetteville: University of Arkansas Press, 1998.

"What Is the Caterpillar Club?" www.caterpillarclub.com (accessed December 29, 2012).

Whiteside, Garrett. "Watching Washington for Thirty-Five Years." *Arkansas Historical Quarterly* 1, 1942.

Whitney, Catherine, et. al. *Nine and Counting.* New York: William Morrow, 2000.

Williams, T. Harry. *Huey Long.* New York: Knopf, 1969.

Wilson, A.L. "'Silent' Hattie Caraway Goes to Washington." *Arkansas Democrat-Gazette,* August 1, 1999.

"A Woman Presides Over the Senate." www.senate.gov (accessed December 12, 2012).

INDEX

ABOUT THE AUTHOR

HATTIE W. CARAWAY
United States Senator

Dr. Nancy Hendricks holds a doctorate in education, a master's degree in English and a bachelor's in English and theater. She is currently director of alumni communications at Arkansas State University in Jonesboro, where she previously taught English.

Formerly a professional actor, Hendricks is also an award-winning writer whose play *Miz Caraway and the Kingfish* portrays the election of America's first female senator, Hattie Caraway. Its New Orleans production was held over for an extended run and nominated by the American Critics Association for "Best Play Produced Outside New York."

She is the playwright of the dramatization *Dear Mrs. Caraway, Dear Mr. Kays* and is also author of the book of the same name. She appeared in her signature role as Senator Hattie Caraway in the film *Hattie Caraway, the Silent Woman,* which was shown on Arkansas Educational Television. Hendricks also performs a one-person program titled *Hattie to Hillary: Women in Politics.*

She wrote and directed the historical play *Second to None.* Her most recent play is *Boy Hero: The Story of David O. Dodd,* and her screenplay, *Terrible Swift Sword,* about the Sultana disaster, is being perused in Hollywood.

She is a contributing writer for the *Encyclopedia of Arkansas* and for *Disasters and Tragic Events and How They Changed American History*. She is also the author of the children's books *Hello Howl* and *Howl's Journey* and has chaired a national playwriting competition.

A founding member of the National Women's History Museum in Washington, D.C., she is also a member of the Southern Association of Women Historians.

She is the recipient of the Pryor Award for Arkansas Women's History, the Arkansas Governor's Arts Award and the White House Millennium Award for her writing.